GLOBETROTTER™

*Travel Guide*

# DELHI
# JAIPUR AND AGRA

KAPKA KASSABOVA
AND SAGARIKA GHOSE

NEW HOLLAND

P9-CDG-984

NEW
HOLLAND

★★★ Highly recommended
★★ Recommended
★ See if you can

Second edition published in 2005
by New Holland Publishers (UK) Ltd
London • Cape Town • Sydney • Auckland
First published in 2002
10 9 8 7 6 5 4 3 2 1

website: www.newhollandpublishers.com

Garfield House, 86 Edgware Road
London W2 2EA, United Kingdom

80 McKenzie Street
Cape Town 8001, South Africa

14 Aquatic Drive, Frenchs Forest
NSW 2086, Australia

218 Lake Road, Northcote
Auckland, New Zealand

Distributed in the USA by
The Globe Pequot Press, Connecticut

Reproduction by Hirt & Carter (Pty) Ltd, Cape Town
Printed and bound by Times Offset (M) Sdn. Bhd.,
Malaysia.

**Keep us Current**
Information in travel guides is apt to change, which is
why we regularly update our guides. We'd be grateful
to receive feedback if you've noted something we
should include in our updates. If you have new information, please share it with us by writing to the
Publishing Manager, Globetrotter, at the office nearest
to you (addresses on this page). The most significant
contribution to each new edition will receive a free
copy of the updated guide.

**Photographic Credits:**
Anders Blomqvist: cover, pages 4, 9, 10, 12, 13, 18,
24, 25, 26, 27, 30, 38, 39, 41, 42, 43, 44, 45, 47, 52, 53,
57, 62, 67, 68, 70, 74, 75, 76, 77, 80, 83, 84, 85, 94,109,
110, 116, 117, 118, 119, 120; **SCPL/Dorothy Burrows:**
page 56; **SCPL/Graeme Goldin:** page 28; **SCPL/**
**Johnathan Smith:** page 64; **SCPL/Geoffrey Taunton:**
page 7; **Gerald Cubitt:** pages 6, 8, 106, 113; **Gallo**
**Images:** page 87; **Gallo Images/Anthony Cassidy:** title
page; **Gallo Images/Paul Harris:** page 88; **Hutchison**
**Library:** pages 21, 50, 72; **Hutchison Library/ Gail**
**Goodger:** page 115; **Hutchison Library/C. Maurice**
**Harvey:** page 95; **Hutchison Library/Andrew Hill:**
page 20; **Hutchison Library/Christine Pemberton:**
pages 14, 33, 111, 114; **Hutchison Library/Liba Taylor:**
page 96; **Warren Jacobs:** pages 92, 101, 112; **Caroline**
**Jones:** pages 19, 23, 29, 65, 71, 90, 97; **Haike Manning:**
pages 22, 60; **Fiona Nichols:** pages 16, 54, 73, 98, 99,
100, 102, 103; **Christine Osborne Photo Library/**
**C. Milne:** page 11; **Christine Osborne Photo Library/**
**J. Worker:** , page 37; **PhotoBank/Jeanetta Baker:** pages
15, 36; **PhotoBank/ Peter Baker:** pages 34, 46, 49, 55;
**Richard Sale:** page 69; **Nicholas Sumner:** page 51.
[SCPL = Sylvia Cordaiy Picture Library]

ISBN 1 84537 196 8

**Publishing Manager (UK):** Simon Pooley
**Publishing Manager (SA):** Thea Grobbelaar
**DTP Cartographic Manager:** Genené Hart
**Editors:** Jacqueline de Villiers and Tarryn Berry
**Picture Researchers:** Shavonne Johannes, Colleen
Abrahams
**Design and DTP:** Lellyn Creamer
**Cartographer:** Nicole Bannister
**Consultant:** Melissa Shales
**Proofreader:** Claudia dos Santos

**Cover:** *New Delhi's Red Fort, with Jama Masjid in
the background.*
**Title page:** *Five women in festival costume.*

# CONTENTS

# 1
# Introducing
# Delhi, Jaipur and Agra

The **Golden Triangle** of India, made up of **Delhi** at the apex and **Jaipur** and **Agra** at the western and eastern extremities, lies in the heart of north India. It is a **landlocked** region enclosed by the **Himalaya mountains** to the north, the Great Indian or **Thar desert** to the west and the **Aravalli hills** to the south. To the east stretch the teeming fertile plains of the **River Ganges**, endlessly green with fields of wheat, sugar cane, mustard and lentils. Delhi is the capital of India and also has the status of a state. Jaipur is the capital of the state of **Rajasthan** and Agra is the seat of the **Taj Mahal** and an important industrial and tourist centre in the state of **Uttar Pradesh**.

Successive empires have flourished in and around the Golden Triangle, from the ancient civilization of **Mohenjo Daro** and **Harappa** (2500BC–1700BC) west of Rajasthan to the ancient city of **Indraprastha** (1450BC) in Delhi and the powerful Rajput principalities that now make up the state of Rajasthan. Home to no fewer than seven historic cities, Delhi became the capital of the mighty Mughal empire (1526–1858) in which Delhi, Jaipur and Agra were bustling centres of arts and politics. The Golden Triangle evolved in the early 20th century with the arrival of the British; only Jaipur remained a semi-independent principality.

With Independence in 1947, the Golden Triangle became a crucible of politics. During the **freedom struggle**, Uttar Pradesh was the centre of powerful Gandhian movements and after Independence the majority of India's prime ministers came from that state. Modern-

**Opposite:** *Elephant at Amber Fort-Palace.*

**GEOGRAPHY**

The Golden triangle is bound by the fertile green **Gangetic plains** to the east and the **Thar desert** to the west. The Aravalli mountain ranges of central India also extend into parts of Delhi and Rajasthan. Two important rivers – the **Ganges** and the **Yamuna** – flow through the Golden Triangle towards the Bay of Bengal. Delhi, Jaipur and Agra are situated on flat land, dotted with rocky out-crops. Rajasthan is a desert area and the soil is sandy and dry. Agra is situated in the plains of the Ganges; Delhi in the north is close to the foothills of the Himalayas.

day Jaipur, subsumed into the new country along with the rest of Rajasthan, is a shadow of its former glory, but nonetheless remains far more than an '**open air museum**' that shows off the art and architecture of the once-powerful Rajput kingdoms. Delhi's position as India's capital makes it a showcase for the country's richly layered history and society. The seven cities of Delhi (some say 15) make up a long chain of historic urban centres, of which New Delhi – built by the British between 1911 and 1939 – is the most recent. However, the current rapid expansion of Gurgaon south of the city could herald the arrival of the next.

The Golden Triangle is at a cultural vantage point between Hindu, Muslim and Western religions. The traditional and the modern face each other on every noisy colourful street corner. Muslim and Hindu, upper caste and gypsy swarm down the streets and into holy places. Opel Astras and bullock-carts pause together at traffic lights. Jean-clad young professionals climb up temple stairs. A caparisoned elephant might be brought in to celebrate the launch of a new software company, while the call of the muezzin competes with Hindu bells.

## THE LAND

**Below:** *A typical street scene in Old Delhi, bustling with taxis and rickshaws.*

Every invader or traveller who galloped into India through the high passes in the northwest frontier, passed through this area and it is strategically vital for the control of the rich **Gangetic plain** as well as access to the trade routes of the **Gulf of Kutch**. Rajasthan is rugged terrain. The shifting sands of the desert are set aflame by the sun during the day and at night the clear desert air provides a magnificent view of the stars. Western Rajasthan is the *maru* or desert, but eastern Rajasthan is fertile with irrigated valleys that are home to the cities of Jaipur and the lake city of **Udaipur**. Delhi is situated on the banks of the **Yamuna River**, a tributary of the Ganges, and lies roughly in the centre of north India. It is bordered by the Aravalli mountain ranges in the south with a shaky backbone, called the **North Ridge**, extending to the north. 223km (139 miles) from Delhi lies Agra, the capital of the Mughal empire from 1526 to 1648.

**Above:** *Buffaloes enjoying a dip in the Yamuna River.*

Agra is also situated on the banks of the Yamuna and is surrounded by the agricultural land known as the *braj-bhumi* (the ancient birthplace of the Hindu god Krishna). The towns of **Vrindavan** and **Mathura**, situated in the *braj*, are places of Hindu pilgrimage. The lush green of the Yamuna, south and west past Agra, gives way to the hot stony ravines of the **River Chambal**. This staggering landscape was once *dacoit* (gang) country. After the decline of the Mughals small kingdoms emerged here.

## Flora and Fauna

Many varieties of flowers bloom throughout the summer monsoon: there are among others marigold, begonias, chrysanthemums, poinsettias, nasturtiums, phlox and calendulas. New Delhi is lined with trees, such as tamarind, *amalta* (yellow-flowering), *neem* (medicinal), *jamun* (a tree with black berries) and *peepul* (a tree with large leaves useful for shade). Fluttering in Delhi's parks are many birds, such as sparrows, crows, kites, parrots, pigeons, as well as the grey hornbills, lapwings, babblers, *mynahs*, *papeehas* and *koels* (song birds), tree pies, magpie robins and golden orioles.

Occasionally, Delhi's streets are dignified by a visiting camel or elephant from Jaipur – either for a grand wedding or a fair – plodding loftily among the groups of placidly confident cattle which graze on Delhi's traffic islands or curl up for a nap in the traffic flow.

### CLIMATE

Since the Golden Triangle is a landlocked area, the temperatures are extreme. In summer, particularly in May, June and July, the sun is ferocious and the heat is almost murderous, particularly when accompanied by the *aandhi*, a hot dry dust storm. In winter, notably December and January, the weather can turn quite cold and smoggy. The monsoon is usually unpredictable and can come any time between July and September. September is muggy and hot. The best time to visit the Golden Triangle is between October and March when the weather is cool and dry. January can be chilly and wet. February is the flowering month when the parks in Delhi and Agra begin to bloom. By March you can sense the onset of the great heat.

**Above:** *The tiger is a threatened species.*
**Opposite:** *From the Mahabharata: Krishna and Indra in battle.*

The **Sultanpur Bird Sanctuary**, 46km (29 miles) west of Delhi, is situated around a shallow *jheel* (lake). There are several pretty walks around it offering a sight of grandly flapping wings of the Sarus crane – the world's largest flying bird – or twinkling kingfishers.

Birds and animals were once the target for the hunting parties of sultans and viceroys. *Shikar* (hunting) was an important flourish of all India's rulers, whether Hindu, Islamic or British. Now, wildlife conservation initiatives like **Project Tiger** have resulted in strict laws on hunting. A famous film star was recently prosecuted for killing black buck. In the Golden Triangle you can see camels, elephants, the Siberian crane, the Nilgai deer, *sambhar*, spotted deer and tiger.

**Bharatpur** in eastern Rajasthan is renowned for the **Keoladeo Ghana National Park**, a former royal hunting preserve, which has been declared a world heritage site and is one of the world's best bird sanctuaries although now sadly under threat as its wetlands dry up. The name comes from a **Shiva temple** in a dense *ghana* (forest). The park is spread over 29km² (11 square miles), and attracts over 375 bird species belonging to 56 families. Keoladeo is well worth a visit as a magnificent variety of birds can be seen, including the peregrine falcon, steppe eagle, garganey, teal and white ibis. Egrets, darters, cormorants, grey herons and storks hatch thousands of chicks here every year. The Siberian crane, now an endangered species, also migrates here. Wandering among the tall grass and wetlands of Keoladeo you can also see the Nilgai, the largest of the Asian deer, with their characteristic broad backs. At **Sariska National Park**, 107km (66 miles) from Jaipur and 200km (124 miles) from Delhi, you may be lucky enough to see a tiger during the day, although evenings are the best time to spot wildlife. You can also see tigers at **Ranthambhore National Park** near Bharatpur; there are about 45 tigers and a considerable bird population.

---

**POPULATION**

India covers a total area of 3,287,263km² (1,268,884 sq miles). The population of India is over one billion. Delhi has a population of about 13 million. Agra has 1.5 million and Jaipur 2.5 million.

# HISTORY IN BRIEF

The history of the Golden Triangle is also the story of the rise and fall of empires suffused with colourful local legends and folklore.

Through the ages, Delhi was a prize fought over by different empires. It remains a symbol of power for Indians. In fact, the rest of India, in a way, suffers from a 'Delhi complex'. If you talk to people in other cities in the south and east they will tell you how much they resent the pre-eminence of Delhi. But Delhi has been an important centre of political control and social change for at least five centuries.

The history of Delhi begins with the Hindu epic, the Mahabharata, which tells the story of five brothers – the Pandavas – who established a city called **Indraprastha** on the banks of the Yamuna in 1450BC. Since then seven – some say 15 – cities were built on this spot by **Rajputs**, **Turks** and the **Mughals**. The last city of Delhi was built by the British, but they ruled here for only 16 years.

Jaipur's story is part of the history of the Rajputs. It became the formal capital when the modern state of Rajasthan was formed in 1956. The Rajputs of Rajasthan, or '**Rajputana**' as it was called then, were warrior clans who traced their descent from the sun and moon. They emerged in the sixth and seventh centuries and were such fierce fighters that no ruler of Delhi, be it Mughal or British, could ignore them. The relationship between the Rajputs and the Mughals is a long history of rebellion and subsequent alliance. The rulers of **Jaipur** were the **Kachhawahas**, one of the Rajput warrior clans who settled in the Jaipur region and built the magnificent cities of **Amber** and **Jaipur**.

> ### THE RAJPUTS
>
> The Rajputs are believed to have emerged in the 6th and 7th centuries AD. They trace their descent from the sun and the moon and are divided into several warrior clans. They are like the knights of medieval Europe they pride themselves on their gallantry, honour and chivalry. The Rajputs carved out kingdoms in the Rajasthan region and certain clans came to be associated with particular towns, such as the Kachhawaha clan of Jaipur. Today, the Rajputs run luxury hotels in Rajasthan or sit in parliament, but ask any Rajput and he will tell you of the valiant heritage of his family and how they stood up to all their foes. Their surnames are generally Singh (like the Sikhs) and although they never have beards they do, on occasion, sport a huge handlebar moustache!

अर्जुन को गीता का उपदेश          देते हुए श्री कृष्ण

### THE CASTE SYSTEM

Hindu society is divided into a bewildering array of castes. Most Hindus can tell each other's caste from their surnames. Castes originally began as a division of labour, and even today the caste of a person can lead to severe discrimination. Originally the caste system was divided into *brahmins* (priests) at the top, *kshatriyas* (warriors and administrators) next, then *vaishyas* (traders and business-men) and last the *shudras* (menial labourers). Those even lower than labourers were considered to be outside the caste system and were called the Untouchables (*dalits*, see panel, page 11). Each of these broad categories of caste is further subdivided into a number of subcategories. Caste is a highly politicized and sensitive issue today.

Agra, imperial capital of Mughal rulers like **Babur**, **Akbar** and **Jahangir**, reflects the splendour of the Mughals, emperors so powerful, rich and grand that they have given the name, mogul, to Hollywood's mega film producers. The Mughals patronized the arts, music, garden design, jewellery and even cooking, and were tolerant of other religions. The city of **Vrindavan** (forest of fragrant basil) became an important pilgrim centre during Mughal rule when **Chaitanya Mahaprabhu** revived the Krishna cult. In addition to the splendid mosques and tombs of the Mughals – of which the **Taj Mahal** is the best example – the Golden Triangle also offers a historical aspect in the form of several important Hindu temples. For centuries, Muslims and Hindus co-existed here in relative peace, while Akbar went as far as marrying a Muslim, a Hindu and a Christian and form-ing his own new hybrid religion, Din-i-Ilahi.

## Muslim Invasions

The first Islamic 'invaders' of India were the Turks. **Mahmud of Ghazni**, a conqueror from Kabul, raided India many times, including the rich temple of Somnath. After his death in 1033, **Mohammad Ghori** from Afghanistan raced into India and carved out an empire. After Ghori's death, **Qutab-ud-din-Aibak** became the first Sultan of Delhi. In the 12th century Aibak defeated the local Rajput ruler, **Prithviraj Chauhan**, and established the **Delhi Sultanate**. This famous defeat of 1191 has been described in Indian poems and songs and was the first event to begin the long reign of the cen-tral Asians over parts of India.

Five dynasties of Sultans made up the **Sultanate**: the **slaves** the **khalji**, the **tughluqs**, the **sayyids** and the **lodis**. They ruled between 1206 and 1526, before the last Lodi Sultan was defeated at the famous **Battle of Panipat** in **1526** by the colourful

**Below:** *Shah Jahan and Mumtaz Mahal, the story behind the Taj Mahal.*

Turkish conqueror **Babur of Farghana**. During the time of the Sultanate, the **Turks** and **Rajputs** formed rival bases of power, the Turks in the area around Delhi and the Rajputs in the area of Rajputana. The Rajputs were divided into 36 houses or clans such as the **Mewar**, **Marwar** and **Amber**.

## The Great Mughal Empire

The reasons for this conflict between Rajputs and the rulers of Delhi was trade. Every ruler of north India needed to have access to the **Gulf of Kutch** which opened the **sea route** to west Asia. The fertile soil of Gujarat in the west produced a rich cotton crop which was extremely valuable, but from the plains of north India access to Kutch and Gujarat lay through Rajputana. To secure this route, the sultans had to wage war with the Rajputs and for 350 years the two sides remained locked in battle. They were finally defeated in **1527** at the **Battle of Khanua** by the Mughals and never again united under a single banner. After Khanua, a number of shrewd Rajput houses sought alliances with the Delhi rulers. The height of the alliance was reached in the reign of the far sighted Mughal emperor **Akbar** (1556–1605) who co-opted the powerful Rajput princes into the Mughal ruling system.

Babur was the founder of the Mughal dynasty in India. Of him, the British historian Lane-Poole writes, '*The blood of the two great scourges of Asia,* **Timur the Lame** *and* **Ghengiz Khan** *mixed in his veins and to the daring and restlessness of the nomad tartar, he joined the culture and urbanity of the Persian.*' Babur ruled from 1526–30. But it was his grandson who took the Mughal empire to glory.

Akbar inherited only a tiny piece of territory stretching between Delhi and Agra, and parts of Rajputana. But half a century later, he handed over to his son **Jahangir** a dominion that spanned from **Kabul** in the west to **Bengal** in the east, from **Kashmir** in the north to parts of the **Deccan** in the south. Akbar built a complicated and mighty state with the Golden Triangle at its core. He

**Above:** *A memorial to Rajiv Gandhi, adorned with a marigold lei.*

### THE UNTOUCHABLES

The Untouchables or *dalits* were at the very bottom of the Indian social ladder. There are about 170 million *dalits* in India today, still subject to horrifying discrimination. In villages, they are assigned segregated areas to build their homes. Untouchables were called *harijans* or 'children of god' by Gandhi who campaigned for their rights all his life. Traditionally, the Untouchables cleaned people's toilets. Their presence was regarded as 'polluting' by all Hindus, and some orthodox Hindus used to bathe if an untouchable's shadow fell on them. After independence, 22.5% of the seats in Parliament were reserved for Untouchables. Today, *dalits* are becoming ministers and even president of India. However most *dalits* continue to be extremely poor and illiterate.

**Right:** *Akbar's impressive tomb in Sikandra.*
**Opposite:** *A portrait of the liberal Mughal Emperor Akbar.*

## THE MUGHALS

The Mughals sat on the throne of India from 1526 to 1858 but the Great Mughals ruled from 1526 to 1707. After 1707 the kings were weak and decadent. The six great Mughal monarchs were Babur, Humayun, Akbar, Jahangir, Shah Jahan and Aurangzeb. The Great Mughals were conquerors, patrons of the arts and successful administrators and their period is known in Indian history as a time of great achievement, not only in art and architecture but also in statecraft and economic management. The Mughals had colourful romances with their queens and courtesans, they drank a lot and used excessive amounts of opium. All of them, with the exception of Aurangzeb (the last Great Mughal) were liberal and accepting of other religions.

promulgated the doctrine of *sulh-i-kul* (peace to all) a civic religion which teaches personal religion as being subsumed in a higher duty to the state and government. Presiding over an empire with vast differences in religious beliefs, Akbar created an overarching umbrella that gave the empire a pluralist face. As part of his strategy of co-option he invited the Rajput nobility into the ruling elite.

Akbar is regarded as one of the great statesmen of India. The Rajputs bowed to him. **Raja Bhara Mal** of Amber realized that the Mughals were too powerful to fight and concluded an alliance with them. Raja Man Singh, Bhara Mal's grandson, became one of Akbar's most trusted lieutenants. Akbar even married a Rajput princess, **Jodhai Bai**. Only the House of Mewar continued to resist the Mughals.

The history of the Rajput house of **Mewar** in Rajputana, with its capital at **Chittor** and its three rulers **Rana Kumbha**, **Rana Sunga** and **Rana Pratap**, illustrates the legendary valour of the Rajputs as well as their fierce attachment to honour and self-sacrifice. *Jauhar (*or the practise of self-immolation) is when a queen jumped into a funeral pyre if her prince had been defeated in battle and *sati* is when a widow jumps (or is helped) into the funeral pyre with her dead husband. Although strictly illegal, *sati* is still sometimes practised even today. The beautiful queen **Padmini of Mewar** is said to have committed *jauhar* when her husband **Rattan Singh** was defeated by **Sultan Alauddin Khilji** early in the 14th century. Rana Pratap's name is synonymous in Indian history with bravery and defiance of Delhi's rule. Pratap was the only Rajput whom even Akbar could not subdue for a long time, although he was finally defeated at the famous **Battle of Haldighati** in 1576. There were Mughal 'emperors' right up to the time of the 1857 Indian Uprising, although they did not have an empire.

## The British in India

By the 17th century the **British** had arrived in India. The **East India Company** established major ports at Madras and Calcutta in the east, and Surat and Bombay in the west. In 1614, **Sir Thomas Roe**, envoy of **James I**, had arrived at the court of Jahangir offering to negotiate a trading agreement between the Mughal empire and the Company. Soon the British, taking advantage of feuds between Indian rulers and the decline of the Mughals, had become an influential political force. In 1774 **Warren Hastings** became the first governor general of British India.

**A GREAT SOUL**

**Mohandas Karamchand Gandhi** was not a simple man. Born in 1869, he was the son of the hereditary Prime Minister of Kathiawar, trained as a barrister in London and moved to South Africa, where his political career was jumpstarted by the racism he encountered. He returned to India in 1915, launched the first campaign of civil disobedience in 1920, and by 1921 had adopted the signature white *dhoti* (loincloth) worn by the untouchables. His powerful civil protests and spiritual leadership worked with the more overtly political Nehru to achieve Indian independence. He was assassinated by a Hindu extremist in Delhi in 1948.

By the 18th century Mughal power, which had seen efflorescence under Akbar and his grandson **Shah Jahan** (builder of the Taj Mahal), had begun to wane. The last Great Mughal, **Aurangzeb**, presided over a stretched empire, increasingly vulnerable to blood feuds between rival claimants to the throne. Aurangzeb, a cruel, autocratic ruler, murdered his older brother **Dara Shikoh** and imprisoned his father Shah Jahan to acquire the throne. The empire was now under attack from the **Marathas**, a sturdy band of warriors from western India. The Marathas had also been plundering the Rajput kingdoms. In desperation the princes turned to the British. In the early 19th century, the house of Jaipur made an alliance with the British. They signed treaties giving up their independence in return for British protection. Other Rajput houses followed suit and **British residents** were installed in the Rajput palaces. The British also conquered Delhi and Agra at the same time.

The Mughal empire was now in a pathetic state, reduced to the precincts of the **Red Fort** in Delhi. The later Mughals were weak rulers and the last Mughal emperor's name has become a byword of political decline in modern India. His name is **Bahadur Shah Zafar** and he died, in 1862 in **Burma**, in exile, blind and without an empire.

**Below:** *Coronation Park is a resting place of old British Statues, George V on the left.*

## Independence

In 1857 the British faced a crucial test. The **War of Independence** (Bengal Rebellion or **Sepoy Mutiny of 1857**) was a turning point for the British empire in India. A rumour spread that the bullets issued to soldiers were greased with pig or cow fat. All across north India, Hindu and Muslim sepoys rose against the rule of the Company, followed by many others. **Rani Laxmibai of Jhansi**, warrior queen and accomplished equestrian, became famous at this time. The uprising was finally crushed by a small British force led by the heroic **Brigadier General Nicholson** who died in battle. In 1858 India was placed under the direct governorship of the Crown and Victoria became an empress. In 1911, at the famous **Delhi Durbar**, **George V** announced to an audience of 561 maharajahs and a dazzling display of elephants, jewels and Rolls Royce cars that the capital of India was to be shifted from Calcutta to New Delhi.

A few years later the Indian freedom struggle began in earnest. The **Indian National Congress** had already been formed in 1885. In 1915 **Mohandas Karamchand Gandhi** (or *Mahatma,* meaning Great Soul) arrived in India from **South Africa**. By 1920 Gandhi had become the supreme symbol of the Indian freedom struggle. Travelling third class, speaking simple Hindi and wearing only a loin cloth, he converted the freedom movement from a genteel group of upper class negotiators – most of them lawyers educated in England – to a massive passionate movement across India. Thousands joined his movement of *satyagraha* (war for truth) and *ahimsa* or non-violent protest. Huge political movements like the Non-Cooperation agitation of 1922 or the **Civil Disobedience** of 1932 and the **Quit India movement** of 1942 took place under the leadership of Gandhi, Nehru and the Congress Party. In 1945 the Labour government was elected to power in Britain and preparations for handing over

**Above:** *Mahatma Gandhi, leader of a nation.*

### THE EUNUCHS OF INDIA

The eunuchs or transvestites of India, known as *hijras*, are unique and at an estimated half a million, form a substantive, and ancient, subculture and a caste of their own. You may see them in the streets of Old Delhi, in Lodhi Gardens on weekends – or indeed in any other city. They dress as women and some look quite feminine, while others have decidedly male features and body-shapes. Traditionally, the eunuchs were highly valued at the royal courts of the Mughals and were exclusive harem-guardians, often reaching positions of power. The curse of a *hijra* is still widely feared – which is why they make their living from dancing and singing at weddings and births.

*Above: Buildings of the Secretariat, New Delhi.*

independence to India began. On 14 August 1947 the last Viceroy of India, **Lord Mountbatten**, handed over power to the Indian National Congress. India was partitioned, Pakistan was created and Delhi became the capital of independent India. The first prime minister, **Jawaharlal Nehru** made his famous speech about India's '**tryst with destiny**' from the ramparts of the Red Fort in Delhi. The freedom movement has been greatly mythologized in modern India and this emotional speech is taught in every school across the country.

The independence and partition of India and the subsequent creation of Pakistan saw unprecedented **religious riots** and **mass killings**. As soon as the new borders were announced, 10 million Hindus, Muslims and Sikhs fled from their homes in India and Pakistan. Around one million died fighting. In the same year, the state of Jammu and Kashmir was invaded by Pakistani forces. Thus began the long and blood-stained dispute over **Kashmir** between India and Pakistan that continues to take a heavy toll of human life to this day. On 30 January 1948 a Hindu fundamentalist shot and killed Gandhi. With the great leader died his treasured politics of non-violence.

## GOVERNMENT AND ECONOMY

India is the world's largest democracy where even the poorest and the illiterate have a vote. While this gives hope to many, it has also led to some peculiar Indian practices such as the emergence of 'vote banks', or enclaves of voters who vote according to ethnic or community loyalties, and the increasing importance of **caste** as a means of political organization. Today, caste identities are very important in politics as castes often vote as a group.

---

**HAWKERS**

Particularly numerous, noisy and tiring in tourist areas, hawkers try to sell cheap kitsch to tourists. If you wish to buy a miniature plastic Taj Mahal, a toy snake, or bangles, make it clear that you are only purchasing this particular item, otherwise you might be trampled by other hopefuls. If you wish to buy, bargain hard. If you do not wish to buy anything, make that clear, too, by saying 'No, thank you' politely, but emphatically. They will pursue you until you get the message across or until they find another victim and lose interest in you.

India's democracy is robust and colourful and although there has been a ban on loud speakers and decorations during elections since 1996, a carnival atmosphere pervades at this time. Astrologers, wrestlers, folk dancers and street performers are all roped in to further electoral fortunes. Incidents of violence, **booth capturing** and **proxy voting** are also common.

The transportation of ballot boxes from remote areas to counting centres has been the subject of many photo-essays. Ballot boxes may be transported on the backs of elephants or by boat, or by camel-drawn carts through the desert to reach remote villages in the interior!

The Indian Constitution, announcing a **Sovereign, Secular, Socialist Republic** came into force in 1950. The event is celebrated every year with grand Republic Day parades in all major cities, generally showing off India's military might and floats of its traditional culture. The president is the head of state, the prime minister is the head of government. There is a two-house parliament. The *Lok Sabha* is the House of the People with 545 seats. The *Rajya Sabha* is the Council of States with 250 seats. Every state capital follows the same structure with a *Vidhan Sabha* (Lower House) and a *Vidhan Parishad* (Upper House). Most large Indian villages have village councils known as *panchayats*. The panchayat is often the arena where a number of politicians cut their teeth before they can contest state elections. If popular enough, they are given tickets for the national elections. The politician-criminal nexus or role of thuggery and corruption is high in the Indian political scene where some candidates even contest election from prison.

**Jawaharlal Nehru**, the first prime minister, died in 1964 and was replaced by **Lal Bahadur Shastri**. When Shastri died, Nehru's

> ### GOVERNMENT
>
> India is a **socialist** and **secular** republic with 28 states and 7 union territories. The government of India is a federation of **democratically elected** state governments. Head of State is the **president**, but political control resides with the **prime minister**, appointed by members of the majority parliamentary party. This is currently the Congress Party, closely followed by the BJP (Bharatiya Janata Party). The President is Abdul Kalan, the Prime Minister, Manmohan Singh.

**Below:** *The dream of independence, India's first national flag.*

## RICKSHAWS

The best mode of transport in Old Delhi, Jaipur and Agra, bicycle rickshaws go shorter distances and are cheaper than auto-rickshaws, although bigger bums should pay more. In rush-hour traffic they are, however,not the safest. Bear in mind that rickshaw drivers may take you to particular shops – usually not the best deal – where they get a commission. Ignore them and tell them exactly where you want to go. Some drivers make very good guides, especially if you find an English-speaking one to take you around the narrow streets of Old Delhi. Tip extra for guide service.

**Below:** *Jawaharlal Nehru, the first Prime Minister.*

daughter, **Indira Gandhi**, who is criticized for being autocratic and not as visionary as her father, was elected to succeed him. The Congress party split in 1969, and Indira Gandhi became leader of the Congress. She declared the **Emergency** in 1975, was ousted in 1977 and won a landslide victory in 1980. She was gunned down by her Sikh bodyguards in 1984 after she ordered the controversial storming of the **Sikh** religious **shrine**, the Golden Temple. Riding a huge sympathy wave, her son **Rajiv Gandhi** swept the polls in the largest mandate in Indian history, but lost the 1989 elections to **VP Singh** after scandals regarding the purchase of the Bofors gun from a Swedish company. Singh commissioned the infamous **Mandal Commission Report** allowing the reservation of government jobs for those classified as backward castes. This report set in motion a movement of the assertion of backward caste demands, which is becoming ever more powerful today. In 1990, **Chandrashekhar** replaced Singh. In the run-up to the 10th general elections, Rajiv Gandhi was assassinated by a **Tamil suicide bomber** as a result of his having ordered an **Indian Peace Keeping Force** to intervene in the civil war between Tamils and Sinhalas in **Sri Lanka**. After Rajiv's death, the Congress Party limped to power and prime minister **PV Narasimha Rao** formed a minority Congress government.

In 1991 this government initiated the liberation of India's economy by starting to dismantle the socialist economy and introducing free-market reforms. After the 1996 elections the **Bharatiya Janata**, a broadly right-wing Hindu nationalist party, briefly formed a government, to be replaced by two others in quick succession lead by Deve Gowda and IK Gujral. In the1999 elections, the Bharatiya Janata Party and its allies came into power.

The Bharatiya Janata Party (BJP) achieved national prominence after the demolition of the **Babri Masjid** mosque in

Ayodhya, said to stand on the site of a Rama temple, in 1992. Since then the BJP has been associated with majoritarian Hindu sentiments, an image it is now trying to live down by appealing to broader sections of the population. In recent years, the emergence of regional parties like the Telegu Desam of **Andhra Pradesh**, **Trinamool Congress** in West Bengal and the **AIADMK** and **DMK** in Tamil Nadu have considerably blunted the power of the older national parties. However, in 2004, Congress Party regained power during the national elections, its campaign spearheaded by Rajiv Gandhi's charismatic Italian widow, Sonia. Most expected her to become prime minister and continue the Nehru dynasty, but she stepped aside in favour of Manmohan Singh.

**Above:** *Bicycle rickshaw at the Red Fort.*

Delhi is currently controlled by Congress, Rajasthan by the BJP, and Uttar Pradesh by the Samajwadi Party (Equality and Prosperity), a strong believer in capitalism and foreign investment.

Left-wing structures like the **Communist Party of India** (CPI) and the **Communist Party of India [Marxist]** (CPI[M]) do not get too many votes but are influential lobbying and pressure groups.

Although Lucknow is state capital, Agra plays an important part in the politics of **Uttar Pradesh**, which is India's most politically significant state, as it sends the largest number of members to the parliament of the *Lok Sabha*.

Caste is an important social division in Uttar Pradesh. The upper castes generally vote for the BJP while the lower ones vote for parties like the **Bahujan Samaj Party** (BSP) or **Samajwadi Party** (SP). The political emergence of the *dalits* or Untouchables and their own party – the BSP – has been one of the most phenomenal developments in recent times, as India's politics have traditionally been dominated by the upper castes.

### GHATS

Ritual bathing in holy water is an important part of Hindu belief. Ghats are steps that lead down into rivers or lakes and each one is given its own name. The word comes from the Hindi *ghati* which means valley. The stairs leading down into the water are seen as valleys leading into the river. The ghats that line the Ganges are considered spiritually important and a number of temples are situated along this river. Pilgrims descend these steps to bathe in the holy water and to take some home with them. You will also see *sadhus* meditating, smoking *ganja* (marijuana) or just praying to the sun rising above the river. Alarmingly, some are also used as cremation grounds, with ashes and even bodies then given to the sacred waters – amongst the bathers.

**Above:** *Republic Day celebrations at India Gate.*

---

**THE GRAND TRUNK ROAD**

The Grand Trunk or GT Road is one of the oldest in India. It runs across India from Amritsar in the west to Calcutta in the east, and links Agra and Delhi. Along its length, you can see the Mughal *kos minars* (milestones) all of them now protected monuments and ringed by railings. The Mughals also built *serais* or rest houses along this road. Some of these rest houses became important centres of trade and it is said that even emperors stayed here when they travelled. Nobody quite knows when the original Grand Trunk Road was built, but every ruler added his own touch. In British times the road was redesigned significantly to include Varanasi.

The GT is busy and provides a perfect snapshot of Indian road life. It also features significantly in Rudyard Kipling's novels, particularly in *Kim*.

---

**Rajasthan** is a recent addition to the political map of India. It was only created in 1956, with Jaipur as its capital, when the privy purses of the princes were abolished. After the British left, their paramountcy over the princely states of Rajputana lapsed and the states were left technically free of all control and without relationship with the rest of India. The merging of all the little principalities of Rajputana took a long time and only after the strenuous efforts by the country's first home minister, **Sardar Vallabhai Patel**, did the princes agree to accept the sovereignty of independent India. The **maharajahs**, stripped of their riches and powers, are mute spectators to the new democracy. The present head of the Kachhawaha dynasty is **Maharajah Bhawani Singh** (or Bubbles, as he is called because of the amount of champagne drunk at the time of his birth). His father, **Man Singh II**, was one of the most anglicized of all Rajputs, and a keen collector of vintage cars. Many modern Rajput princes are educated, at least in part, in the UK.

## Economy

**Reforms** to change the socialist-style planned economy were introduced in 1991. They generated huge increases in private investment and boosted exports and imports, but they were also inconsistent and created social unrest. The objective of the reforms was to reduce the role of the public sector in heavy manufacturing, banking, telecommunication and power generation, but there is still a long way to go. Today, fringe groups like the right-wing Swadeshi Jagran Manch as well as the left oppose economic reforms. Indian industrialists continue to demand a level playing field, ie. equal benefits for foreign and domestic companies.

India's main exports are **gems**, **jewellery**, **cotton yarn** and **fabrics**, **handicrafts**, **engineering goods**, **chemicals** and **leather goods**. The last few years have shown remarkable economic progress with real signs of prosperity and the government talking of overtaking the UK within 10 years. However, the huge numbers of people employed by the government are heavily unionized and resist any attempts at streamlining. Economists claim that reforms are taking place only in the big cities while the rest of the country remains consigned to agrarian backwardness.

**Agriculture** is no longer the main economic activity in India, contributing 23.4% to the Gross Domestic Product, although it employs 60% of the total workforce. India is the world's largest **milk producer** and, at 193 million, has among the largest number of cattle in the world. Cows can be seen wandering on every street in the country. India is the world's largest producer of rice and tea and the fourth largest of **wheat**. It is also a world leader in the **banana**, **mango**, **coconut** and **cashew** market, as well as that of **potatoes**, **tomatoes**, **onions** and **green peas**. It is also one of the world's 10 largest producers of **pineapples** and **apples**. Industry now accounts for 28.4% of GDP and 17% of the workforce. Services provide 48% of GDP although employing only 23% of workers.

The Golden Triangle is a relatively prosperous zone. Benetton, McDonald's and Pepsi outlets are mushrooming in the smaller towns of this region. In Rajasthan there are over 125,000 small-scale industries and over 200 large and medium-sized industries. Rajasthan has invested about 20 billion US dollars in the industrial sector. Delhi is an industrial hub and seat of many multinationals like Adobe, Coca Cola and Pepsi, including several international banks such as ABN Amro and Standard & Chartered Bank. The majority of Delhi's population has come here for economic reasons as the local average wage is double that paid in the rest of the country. Agra, too, is situated in the more prosperous western Uttar Pradesh, a region which is home to industry and mechanized agriculture. The eastern part of Uttar Pradesh is poverty-stricken and very backward.

**Below:** *Drying racks for freshly dyed saris.*

## THE PEOPLE

As in the rest of India, the people of the Golden Triangle are a colourful mix of communities, religions, languages and traditional tribes. All the gradations of the caste system (*see* page 10) are found here: the upper *brahmins* and *kshatriyas*, the middle-ranking *vaishyas* and the lowest, menial labourers. Then there are the Untouchables (*dalits, see* panel, page 11), who do not have a caste and are the the lowest and poorest of them all. Almost all of India's communities are represented in Delhi: dark-skinned **Tamils** and **Keralites**, lighter-skinned **Punjabis**, the shorter, squatter **Bengalis**, as well as **Maharashtrians**, **Gujaratis** and students from the northeastern states of **Assam** and **Nagaland**.

It is interesting to see how certain communities have created their own housing areas in the capital. **Janak Puri** in west Delhi is dominated by Keralites and Tamils, while **Chittaranjan Park** in south Delhi is made up almost entirely by Bengalis. It is complete with a market that stocks a wide variety of delicious fish.

Thousands of migrant labourers from the villages of Bihar, Uttar Pradesh and Haryana swarm into Delhi to look for work. Certain jobs and services have become associated with distinct communities and castes. **Tribal Christian girls** from Bihar work as housemaids, a number of plumbers come from **Orissa**, the nurses from **Kerala**, and the *dosa* (south Indian bread) restaurants are, of course, all staffed by Tamils or Keralites.

In Delhi, you can also see the **puppie**, or Punjabi Upwardly Mobile Professional, zoom by in a Hyundai or Honda and swing in the city's booming nightclubs. India's **Generation X** are called the **trendy**

**Below:** *Smiling children in Jaipur reflect the origins of their forefathers.*

**conservatives**. They dress fashionably and listen to the latest western pop music, but few are able to break out of parental control. Living together, having gay relationships and even divorce are still fairly unacceptable.

In Rajasthan the most visible group are the Rajputs – the warriors rep-

**Above:** *Jaipur City Palace guards with characteristic brightly coloured Rajasthani turbans.*

resenting different noble houses – like the Kachhawahas of Jaipur, the Rathods of Jodhpur and the Sisodias of Mewar. Together with the *brahmins* they constitute less than a tenth of Rajasthan's population. With a brightly coloured turban and handlebar moustache, the Rajput prides himself on his ancestry, although many have now fallen on hard times and have been forced to convert their ancestral properties into luxury hotels. Rajput villagers might be tall and brightly turbaned, but they are also impoverished and skinny.

There are several other communities like the **Marwaris** (traditional traders). One of India's richest industrialist families, the Birlas, are Marwaris. There are tribes like the **Bishnois**, traditional conservationists who have been known to commit suicide in their efforts to protect trees and animals. There are also *banjaras* (gypsies) who wear colourful clothes and **heavily oxidized silver jewellery**. In fact, the highly skilled artisans of Rajasthan are becoming leading couturiers. Their vibrantly coloured **mirror-work fabric**, block-prints, silver jewellery set with semi-precious stones, ornament design and *minakari* jewellery (mirrorwork on gold), as well as *bandhani* print (the tie and dye print, patterned with tiny white squares, circles and lines) are justifiably famous. Most of India's artisans have been practising their art for generations and some, like the celebrated *minakars* (jewellery artisans) of Jaipur trace their descent as far back as the 17th century.

**LITERACY**

Approximately 60% of India is literate – 70.2% of men are literate but only 48.3% of women can read and write. Delhi's literacy rate is 79%. Indians love politics, and political discussions are loudly carried out in *baithaks* (gatherings), *chai* (tea) stalls and roadside *dhabas* (snack stalls). No wonder then that there are around 1800 daily newspapers and an explosion of interest in the Internet and satellite TV.

*Above: The Elephant Festival in Jaipur is one of the best in India.*

Agra has almost the same social landscape as Delhi where Hindu and Muslim have lived as friendly neighbours (and occasional enemies) for centuries. The Agra region is not only known for its Islamic monuments, but also for the Hindu Krishna cult that flourishes around Vrindavan, an important Hindu pilgrim centre north of Agra.

Hindus generally believe in the two epics, (*Ramayana* and *Mahabharata*), the fact that all living beings are manifestations of the Supreme Being or *brahman* and that there are three aspects to God: **Creator** (*Brahma*), **Destroyer** (*Shiva*) and **Preserver** (*Vishnu*). But there are also a huge number of local gods, small shrines and cults, all of which are recognized as Hindu if they are associated with the holy trinity or the two epics.

**Muslims** believe in the Prophet Muhammad's teachings as set down in their holy book, the Qur'an. In India, the **Sufi** or mystical aspects of Islam are also strong. The Sufi (wandering mystic) is known for his personal communion with God. He whirls in ecstasy while praying and is known as a *mast qalandar* (intoxicated by devotion). The shrine of **Khwaja Moinuddin Chisti** in Ajmer is an important centre for the Islamic world. The **Sikhs**, with their main shrine at the Golden Temple in Amritsar, believe in the teachings of their gurus, while **Buddhism** and **Jainism** adhere to doctrines of compassion, non-violence and personal communion with God. They are systems of philosophy and codes of morality that adhere to the achievement of enlightenment.

## Food and Drink

North Indian cuisine is generally called *mughlai* food with a heavy emphasis on barbecued and curried meats and breads and rice eaten with flavoured yoghurt.

---

### FOOD TERMS

*badam* • almond
*dhal* • lentils
*dosa* • crispy rice-pancake
*ghee* • clarified butter
*gulab jamun* • fried Bengali sweet soaked in syrup
*iddli* • steamed rice cake
*lassi* • fresh yoghurt drink (salted or sweetened)
*masala* • spices
*naan* • leavened bread made with yoghurt
*roti* • general term for tandoor-baked bread
*tandoor* • clay oven
*thali* • an all-in-one meal: a platter of vegetarian or non-vegetarian dishes, pickles, rice and bread

A vegetable or non-vegetable *thali* (a metal dish) set with metal *katoris* (bowls), is a full Indian meal consisting of rice, bread, curries, chutneys, *papads* (crispy deep fried wafers), curds and *mithai* (generic term for Indian sweets). *Biryani* (rice flavoured with spices and cooked with chunks of meat or vegetables) and *pulao* (rice mixed with vegetables, lamb or chicken) are also common. Typical vegetable dishes are *sabzi* (mixed vegetable), *baigan bharta* (curried eggplant) and *aloo jeera* (spiced potatoes). Standard non-vegetarian dishes would be butter chicken, *rogan josh* (lamb curry), *gushtaba* (meatballs) or chicken *korma* (curry with curd). *Kebabs* (skewered barbecued meats) are common in Delhi, as are *shammi* (flat kebabs of minced meat), *seekh* (sausages of seasoned lamb) and *burra* (pieces of lamb grilled on a charcoal fire).

Communities like the **Jains** and certain *brahmins* are strict vegetarians. Typical south Indian fare like *dosas* (rice pancakes), *idlis* (steamed rice dumplings) and *sambhar* (savoury lentils) is also completely vegetarian and available all over Delhi and Agra. Roadside stalls dispense cut fruit, *samosas* (fried and stuffed dumplings), *paapri chaat* (savoury pastry chips smothered in curds and chutney) and *chole bhatoore* (spiced chickpeas with fried bread), but these are best avoided. **Delhi belly** (food or water poisoning) can sometimes turn nasty and even locals suffer if they are not careful. *Mithai* (sweets), made from thickened milk and sugar are generally safe. Different types of *mithai* are: *laddoos* (sweet yellow balls), *jalebis* (twisted fried sugar), *gulab jamuns* (cardamom-flavoured caramelized sugar-and-milk balls) and *kulfi* (ice cream).

*Dal* (lentils) and cereal (rice or bread) is the staple diet all across this region. Most Indians eat *achar* (pickles) with their meals. Other side dishes include *dahi* (curd) or *raita*

**PAAN**

You will see people – mostly men – chewing and spitting a blood-coloured substance in the streets. This is produced from chopped betel nut, a mild hallucinogen, with various additives such as white lime, *mitha masala* (sweet spices) and *zarda* (chewing tobacco, which is not to be swallowed), wrapped in a betel leaf. *Paan* is sold in square foil at countless street stalls. For first-time users, the *mitha* variety is recommended as it can safely be ingested. Indians can spit *paan* juice from a mile, sometimes leading the visitor to think they are vomiting blood. A certain type of *paan* is known as the *palang-tod* (wrecker of beds), since it supposedly acts as an aphrodisiac.

**Below:** *Making* naan *in a traditional* tandoor *oven.*

### CHAI

Chai is the Indian tea-brew which is traditionally made by boiling tea leaves with milk, sugar and spices. Sold at every streetstall, café and restaurant, it is delicious and refreshing in any season. It is safe to drink anywhere as the water is always boiled. To purchase top Indian tea, either in bulk or gift-wrapped, as well as various tea accessories at good prices, go to Mittal Tea House at 8-A Main Market, Lodi Colony, New Delhi 110003, tel: 461 5709, 469 2378.

(flavoured curd with cucumber or tomatoes). A common drink is *lassi* or iced yoghurt shake. Indian beer is high in alcohol content and brands like **Kingfisher** and **Haake Beck** are good. Try to avoid brands like **Thunderbolt** that have a ferociously high alcohol content. Many restaurants do not serve alcohol.

## Architecture

The architecture of the Golden Triangle is grand and there are monuments here in the **Hindu**, **Indo-Islamic** and **British colonial** styles.

The Indo-Islamic style is evident in the **Taj Mahal** (*see* page 96) and the other elegant luxuriously carved monuments in Agra. The Taj (proud passion of an Emperor's love) is a beautiful, melancholic monument built by **Shah Jahan**. This Mughal emperor was so devoted to his wife **Mumtaz Mahal**, who died in delivering her child, that he built this memorial to her. Legend has it that the emperor had the thumbs of all the artisans cut off after they finished their breathtaking carvings, so that they would never be able to build another like it ever again. The Mughals used a great deal of **white marble** and **red sandstone** and the Taj is the best example of Mughal style with its elegant minarets and dome, elevated platform, rich carvings and screens.

The decorated forts, tombs and gardens of Agra show Mughal splendour at its height. The **pietra dura** technique (inlaid flowery patterns of semi-precious stones on marble) can also be seen here, as well as the use of running water for cooling. The delicate **Itimad-ud-Daulah's Tomb** in Agra (*see* page 103) is described as a 'jewelbox of marble' and is, to some, even more beautiful than the Taj itself.

The red sandstone desert palace **fortresses** of Rajasthan show the varied styles used by Rajput

**Below:** *Delicious* mithai *are made from thickened milk, sugar and flavouring.*

architects. They are decorated with carved wooden doors, balconies, pillared verandas, mirrors and mosaics, latticed windows, *chhatris* (pavilions), painted walls, tall battlements and domes in the Mughal style. The colonial buildings erected by the British in **Delhi** use a combination of classical western and Indian styles and they are indisputable reminders that this was the capital of British India. There is an interesting area, north of the old city, known as **Civil Lines** where the British used to live.

The geometrically designed **Jaipur** (also known as the Pink City) and the **Jantar Mantar** observatory show the modernism of Jaipur's remarkable founder **Sawai Jai Singh II**.

Modern Indian architecture is higgledy-piggledy, with all manner of styles and constructions juxtaposed on each other. The luxury villas in Delhi and Jaipur are as fanciful as their owners want them to be. Those with the money to build big houses are not too bothered about history. The restoration of old buildings is sadly neglected and beautiful old *havelis* (townhouses) in Old Delhi have been allowed to fall into ruin. Old and new are combined curiously. Chrome-and-glass high-rises stretch glossily behind Lutyens's (the chief architect of New Delhi) colonial buildings. The clamour and traffic of Jaipur obscures its meticulously planned structure.

**Above:** *Floral motif in multicoloured marble, in the Taj Mahal.*

## Crafts

North Indian crafts range from delicate embroidery on cotton to textile design and intricate jewellery manufacture, as well as folk art such as puppet making and creating clay idols for festivals. Agra is renowned for its gold thread and bead embroidery known as *zardozi* and the pietra dura stonework handed down through families since the 17th century. Agra is also the centre of the old Mughal imperial carpet works. Fine carpets are made both here and in Jaipur.

The *karigars* (craftsmen) of Jaipur are proud, skilled artists who have perfected their art over centuries. Textile

**ARCHITECTURAL GLOSSARY**

*bagh* • garden
*chhatri* • cenotaph, tomb/domed pavilion
*chowk* • square, crossroads
*diwan* • hall
*ghat* • steps to a river
*gurdwara* • Sikh temple
*hammam* • bath-house
*haveli* • townhouse with courtyard
*jaali* • latticed stone or marble screen
*mandir* • Hindu temple
*masjid* • mosque
*pol* • fort gate
*zenana* • women's quarters (Hindu)

design is a specialty of the region. The *bandhani* workers, mostly women, transfer designs onto cotton or chiffon by tying yards of cloth. The *ghagra* (flaring skirt), *choli* (short tied top) and *odhni* (veil) make up the typical Rajasthani dress. In Jaipur, shops like **Anokhi** stock typical block-printed cottons. In fact, its owner, Faith Singh, an Englishwoman by birth, has helped to sell the hand- and block-printed designs (*chhapai*) to tourists and internationally. The owners of the popular shop **Fabindia** in Delhi have done the same. It is easy, quick and cheap to get clothes made in cotton or silk as long as you can provide a template to copy.

Jaipur is also the largest ornament-production centre in India and the expert artisans here work on *zari* (silver and gold thread fabric) and *gota* (gold thread material). Emerald design, garnet-setting, stone-cutting, wood-carving as well as the highly skilled *minakari* (enamelled jewellery work) in which tiny pieces of glass are fused on gold, are all practised in Jaipur. Between them, the towns of **Sanganer**, **Barmer** and **Bagru** in Rajasthan produce about 250,000m (275,000 yards) of printed fabric every day. The **Sanganeri** print is very famous, as is Rajasthani silver and *kundan* (expensive stone, essential if you want to look like old Rajput nobility). Rajasthani *jootis* – leather slip-ons, either decorated or plain – pinch cruelly when you begin to wear them and often need to be soaked in oil to fit your feet. Once they are 'broken in' though, they are very comfortable.

The **Crafts Museum** and **Cottage Industries Emporium** in Delhi are good places to see the crafts of north India, from teak furniture, wood, marble and papier-mâché objects to lampshades and lamps, *dhurries*, carpets and fabric. Mughal and Rajput **miniature paintings** are beautiful, renowned for their subtle use of colour and delicate lines.

## FESTIVALS

In the Golden Triangle the main festival is *diwali* (October), which marks the end of summer and the beginning of winter. Fireworks are set off and houses are decorated with candles and clay lamps. *Diwali* is also a celebration of the legend of Rama, the king of ancient times who was exiled from his kingdom but eventually returned to much rejoicing. *Holi*, the festival of colour (March), is another important event, and marks the onset of summer and time of harvest. People dance, drink *bhang* (marijuana-flavoured milk) and throw coloured powders on each other. Other festivals are *Teej*, popular in Rajasthan, when wives return to their parents' homes and buy new bangles and clothes. *Eid* is a Muslim festival and marks the end of the *ramazan* (fasting period). At the feasts during this time, kebabs, breads and sticky semolina pudding are eaten. *Janamashtami* (October) is a festival marking the birth of the Hindu god Krishna.

## Culture

The culture of India at this time is in a state of enormous flux, with influences from the West being absorbed and resisted at the same time. Indians are looking at their traditional culture and examining it in the light of the new, but the power of the old achievements in *kathak* and *bharatanatyam* (**classical Indian dance**), Urdu **poetry**, Hindi **literature**, traditional vocals and instruments continues and is still very much alive, even though, some classical exponents have been criticized for 'going popular'. The number of Indians writing English literature continues to grow. The trend of dynamic artistic writing in English which began with **Salman Rushdie**'s *Midnight's Children* was taken forward by writers like Amitav Ghosh and Vikram Seth. After **Arundhati Roy's** *The God of Small Things* won the Booker Prize in 1997, a host of other younger writers like Pankaj Mishra, Raj Kamal Jha, Kiran Desai and Jayshree Mishra emerged. Increasingly, the literature and music of the south and northeast of the country are being revived and Delhi is a lively cultural centre that often holds shows, exhibitions and book readings. 'Bollywood', the largest film industry in the world, pumps out its melodramatic song-and-dance performances and some smash box office hits. Younger film-makers are beginning to explore themes like the Mumbai underworld and political corruption.

Home-grown television soaps, new cable channels that show Baywatch and Ally McBeal, and 24-hour news bulletins, lively Internet sites and the fact that an increasing number of Indians are going abroad for education and jobs, places India at a fascinating stage in its history.

> **BEGGARS**
>
> For the first-time visitor, beggars can be a shock. Beggars in tourist spots, many of them children, are bound by a mafia-style dependency and have to give away most of their earnings to their 'boss'. If you want to do some good, ignore the beggars and instead give donations to those charities working with street people. If they are not successful, it may encourage their parents to send them to school, with the prospect of a better life

**Opposite:** *A beautifully adorned Rajastani woman.*
**Below:** *A cinema.*

# 2
# Delhi

At first glance, Delhi is overwhelming. The contrasts that abound on its streets today are as extreme and fascinating as its violent but glorious history. Delhi is an unparalleled experience – Connaught Place and its cacophonous traffic jumble of rickshaws, jeeps, street vendors and pedestrians; Old Delhi's narrow lanes with their entangled telephone wires, strong aromas wafting up from boiling pots, goats and drooling cows; ragged beggars at traffic lights and the slums around the railway station where life goes on with a vitality and dignity that is incomprehensible to the outsider; New Delhi with its elegant mansions, luxury hotels, top restaurants and chic shopping emporia – however you choose to spend your time in this city, the experience is bound to remain deeply etched in your memory.

## THE SEVEN CITIES OF DELHI

'Delhi has many gates of entry but none for departure'
This local saying is validated by the dramatic history of this ancient city. Century after century, Delhi has risen from the ashes of invasions and massacres to blossom again in renewed beauty and glory, and become the multi-layered, vast metropolis that it is today. Depending on your personal preference and schedule, it is possible to spend time in the capital simply soaking up the beguiling atmosphere and enjoying the sights and sounds of a complex culture – there is always something happening on the streets, there is much to taste, hear and see. Alternatively, you can choose to dig deeper through

**DON'T MISS**

\*\*\* **Janpath market:** see a range of Rajasthani fabrics, Tibetan crafts and antiques.
\*\*\* **The Red Fort:** explore this huge Mughal fort.
\*\*\* **Jama Masjid:** climb to the top of the mosque for a good view over Old Delhi.
\*\*\* **Chandni Chowk:** take a stroll or rickshaw ride around the narrow, cluttered lanes.
\*\*\* **Nizamuddin village:** visit the shrine, and try a Mughal dinner at Dastarkhwan-e-Karim.
\*\*\* **Hauz Khas:** stroll along the boutique-lined streets.

**Opposite:** *Rickshaw at the walls of the Red Fort.*

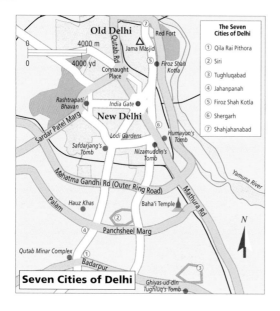

Old Delhi

0    4000 m
0    4000 yd

Red Fort
Jama Masjid
Qutab Rd
Connaught Place
Firoz Shah Kotla
Rashtrapati Bhavan
India Gate
New Delhi
Sardar Patel Marg
Lodi Gardens
Humayun's Tomb
Safdarjang's Tomb
Nizamuddin's Tomb
Mahatma Gandhi Rd (Outer Ring Road)
Yamuna River
Mathura Rd
Palam
Hauz Khas
Baha'i Temple
Panchsheel Marg
Qutab Minar Complex
Badarpur
Ghiyas-ud-din Tughluq's Tomb
N

**The Seven Cities of Delhi**
① Qila Rai Pithora
② Siri
③ Tughluqabad
④ Jahanpanah
⑤ Firoz Shah Kotla
⑥ Shergarh
⑦ Shahjahanabad

**Seven Cities of Delhi**

layers of ruined glory and embark on a rewarding discovery journey through the remnants of a powerful and ever-growing empire, testimony to the extravagant dreams of individual rulers and the reversals of fortune. You will discover that there isn't simply **Old Delhi** and **New Delhi**, but that Delhi consists of no fewer than **seven cities**, the ruins of which (over 20,000 sites in total) lie in the middle of the residential districts known as colonies. If it weren't for the frantic urban expansion that has organically merged with ancient debris, many parts of Delhi would be cordoned off as national heritage sites.

The first settlement in the Delhi area is believed to have been **Indraprastha**, which existed between 1000BC and the fourth century AD and appears in the *Mahabharata* as the beautiful capital built by the Pandava brothers, heroes of the epic. There are no traces of this legendary city today, but the site is marked by the Old Fort or Purana Qila, built by the Afghan king Sher Shah in the 16th century. In the eighth century AD the Tomara Rajputs founded Lal Kot. Four centuries later it was overtaken by another Rajput dynasty – the Chauhans – and became **Qila Rai Pithora**, first city of Delhi, found today in the southern suburb of Mehrauli. There is not much left of the first city as the stones of its many Hindu and Jain temples were used in the construction of the Great Mosque in the **Qutab Minar Complex** nearby to the west. The Rajputs were defeated by invading Afghani troops led by Mohammed Ghuri. This ruler's days were numbered, but his Indian provinces remained under the rule of his Turkish general and ex-slave, **Qutab-ud-din-Aibak**, who founded the enduring Delhi **Sultanate**, beginning with the Slave Dynasty, that marked the advent of Islamic rule over Northern India. He also began the construction of an ambitious project, India's first mosque. **Qutab Minar**, at 73m (238 feet) possibly the highest minaret in the world at the time, proclaimed the supremacy of Islam.

In the late 13th century the Khalji clan of Turks took over from the slave sultans and built the second city of Delhi, **Siri**. The most notable feature of this prosperous city remaining today is the *hauz* or water reservoir, which the Sultan built for the citizens – hence the name of the nearby modern complex of **Hauz Khas**, where some of Delhi's best designer boutiques are found. With the advent of the Tughluq sultans in early 14th century, **Tughluqabad**, the third city of Delhi, came into existence, but was abandoned after only five years due to drought. Mad Sultan Mohammed Tughluq migrated his unwilling citizens 15,000km (9321 miles) to the south of Delhi, but returned a few years later to build **Jahanpanah**, Delhi's fourth city, between Qila Rai Pithora and Siri. The next sultan, Feroz Shah, created **Firoz Shah Kotla**, the fifth city, on the banks of the

> **THE TREES OF NEW DELHI**
>
> The planting of indigenous, long-lived trees was underway even before the construction of New Delhi began. Each avenue has its distinct foliage. Akbar Road has tamarinds whose sour pods are used in cooking. Aurangzeb Road has *neems* whose twigs are traditionally used for toothbrushes. The crossroad of Janpath and Aurangzeb Road has *arjun* trees.

**Below:** *Hauz Khas, once a 13th-century water reservoir.*

Yamuna River. Following a terrible sacking of Delhi by the lame Mongol Taimur who slaughtered 50,000 of its residents, the **Lodi** dynasty ruled with an ever-tightening grip, until a rebellion led by **Babur**, a descendant of Genghis Khan, opened a major chapter in Indian history. The capable Babur became the first **Mughal** ruler. His learned son Humayun was driven out by an Afghan king Sher Shah. who managed to build Purana Qila on the Yamuna – known as **Shergarh** (the sixth city), before Humayun returned and reclaimed his throne. What is today known as Old Delhi is in fact the seventh city, named **Shahjahanabad** after the great emperor Shah Jahan (ruler of the universe) who also built the **Taj Mahal**. His rule was interrupted by his greedy sons of whom the most cunning and also the most unpleasant was Aurangzeb, the next emperor.

Another catastrophic plunder of Delhi occurred in the 18th century when the Persian emperor Nadir Shah invaded India. With the appropriation of Shah Jahan's magnificent Peacock Throne, Nadir Shah signaled the decline of the great Mughal era.

**Right:** *New Delhi, the
President's Palace seen
through the gates.*

The Mughals survived until the bloody mutiny of 1857 when **Bahadur Shah**, the last emperor, was exiled by the British. By then the capital had been shifted to Calcutta, but during his visit to India in 1911, King **George V** of England announced, to everyone's surprise, that the capital was to be moved back. This was to become New Delhi.

## NEW DELHI

With its wide, tree-lined avenues, palatial buildings, foreign embassies, gardens and tidy markets, New Delhi is visitor-friendly and a good place to start your journey. In 1913, noted British architect **Edwin Lutyens** was selected to design the new imperial Delhi. He travelled around North India for inspiration but was impressed by little more than the magical Datia Palace (*see* page 119) and the Buddhist sculptures of Sanchi which also appear in the domes of the **Rashtrapati Bhavan**. After surveying Delhi from elephant-back, Lutyens and his aides decided to build a city 'as an Englishman dressed for the climate'. They proceeded to create an imperial design based on Western classicism, with heterogeneous Indian motifs thrown in, resulting in an imaginative and monumental concoction of styles aspiring to proclaim the supremacy of the British Empire. Lord Hardinge arrived from Calcutta to inaugurate the start of the constructions with a procession along Chandni Chowk where he was injured by a bomb. This added to the various superstitions concerning Delhi.

### GURGAON

Across the state border in Haryana, Gurgaon is rapidly becoming the eighth city of Delhi. In the last few years, this vast building site has turned from a small town to a city of over 1 million, its enormous apartment blocks acting as commuter dormitories for Delhi yuppies. It also has many multinational offices and some of the area's best shopping malls and restaurants.

**Right:** *India Gate, World War I memorial.*

**PARADISE FOR THE PALATE**

Delhi caters for all tastes. In addition to every existing variety of Indian food, you will find excellent Thai, Chinese, Japanese, Middle Eastern, Italian, French and international cuisine. For the unadventurous visitor there are also numerous fast-food restaurants. Depending on your budget and taste you can choose mouth-watering snacks and sweets from the roadside stalls or visit the popular, entertaining and always busy Indian cafés where you can get *dosas*, kebabs, *dal*, *roti*, *lassi* and other tasty staples for a negligible sum. There are also classy restaurants with music and pleasant décor, and exquisite restaurants in the top hotels, some of which rate among the best in Asia.

The cost of the project was extravagant and controversy raged. Thirty thousand labourers were employed, and a railway was built especially for the transportation of building material from the south. By the time it was completed, 500 million tons of material had been carried. Popular leaders Mahatma Gandhi and Nehru commented that such 'vulgar ostentation' was 'in conflict with the best interests of the nation.' But when Lutyens's Delhi was finished, 20 years later, a British historian exclaimed 'I can't describe to you how beautiful it is.'

## Rajpath

Rajpath (Kingsway at the time) is the main axle of Lutyens's capital. At its east end stands the imposing cream-sandstone **India Gate**, Delhi's Arc de Triomphe, an all-India war memorial commemorating the 90,000 Indian soldiers who lost their lives fighting for England in World War I. The names of more than 13,000 Indian and British soldiers killed on the northwest frontier and in the Afghan War of 1919 are inscribed on the arch. An eternal flame burns beneath it for those who died in the Indo-Pakistan War of 1971. Just beyond India Gate is the **Canopy**, the last imperial monument, which housed an imposing statue of George V but is now empty after the statue was exiled to the northern ridge of the city. Looking down Rajpath from India Gate and past the plaza of **Vijay Chowk**, you will see Lutyens's grand achievement – **Rashtrapati Bhavan** with the two **Secretariat Buildings** on each side in perfect symmetry. Built originally as the viceroy's house, Rasthtrapati Bhavan is now the residence of the President of India. Larger than Versailles and containing 340 rooms, this cream and red sandstone edifice with its domes and colonnades is a unique blend of East and West, reminiscent of Mughal tomb, Rajput fortress and colonial palace. In the middle of the court in front of the palace is the **Jaipur Column** built with money donated by the Maharaja of Jaipur. A symbol of victory, the 44m-high (144 feet) column is carved with oak leaves and ends in a bronze lotus from which bursts a crystal star. The Secretariat Buildings, similar in style and grandeur to the Rashtrapati Bhavan, today house the ministries of Foreign Affairs and Finance. In their courtyards are four dominion columns representing Australia, Canada, New Zealand and South Africa, each topped with a globe and a ship.

> **LUTYENS ON INDIAN ARCHITECTURE**
>
> Lutyens, having toured Northern India for inspiration, summed up his opinion of Indian architecture thus: 'Hindu: Set square stones and build child-wise, but before you erect, carve every stone with lace patterns and horrifying shapes. On top – set an onion. Mughal: Build a vast mass of rough concrete, elephant-wise, on a very simple rectangular plan. Inlay jewels and carnelians if you can afford it. Then on top of the mass, put three turnips.' He then proceeded to implement every major Hindu and Mughal architectural trend in his design of New Delhi.

Behind Rashtrapati Bhavan are the beautiful terraced **Mughal Gardens**, open to the public only in February, following Republic Day. Recreating the Mughal quadrant pattern cut by water channels, it has a butterfly garden around a pool, planted with flowers. Today the park employs 150 gardeners, while at the time of its construction 50 staff were employed solely to scare off birds!

To the north of Rajpath and the Secretariat stands Parliament House, **Sansad Bhavan**. With a red sandstone foundation, cream

**Below:** *The South Block of the Secretariat Buildings in New Delhi.*

sandstone middle section and a top storey in plaster (as funds were running short!), this monumental circular construction has 144 colonnades and three semicircular halls that now house the Council of States, the House of the People and a library. The central circular hall with a 28m (90feet) dome is where the Constitution of Independent India was drafted.

### Janpath Market ***

From Rajpath make your way up along **Janpath**, the northsouth artery of Lutyens's Delhi which will take you to **Connaught Place**, the commercial hub of the modern city. Janpath's market is absorbing, so set aside plenty of time for browsing.

Located in a lane off Janpath, it has dazzling authentic Rajasthani textiles sold by a row of hard-bargaining tribal women. If you're prepared to haggle, you won't find the real thing cheaper anywhere else in town. For an orderly, fixed-price selection of the best Indian handicrafts and handlooms – and good service – you can't do better than the two-storeyed **Central Cottage Industries Emporium**, on the corner of Janpath and Tolstoy Marg. If you'd rather browse, the **Tibetan market** has Tibetan jewellery, some real antiques, knick-knacks as well as junk.

**Right:** *Janpath Market in New Delhi.*

## Connaught Place

With its three concentric and seven radial roads that divide it into blocks (from A to N), surrounded by grandiose colonnaded façades, Connaught Place is not just a shopping centre. Named after Duke Connaught, the uncle of King George V, Duke Connaught, it is a worthy addition to Lutyens's parliamentary

**Above:** *The continuous bustle at Connaught Place.*

city, although another architect designed it. The first hotels and cinemas of Delhi were built here. Its busy traffic, street vendors, myriad shops catering for all needs and concentration of hotels and restaurants make it a watershed between modern and Old Delhi. It is best explored on foot or by rickshaw and ideal for window-shopping, lunches and dinners.

Two interesting markets worth perusing are **Palika Bazaar** (between block G and N), which is underground, so it's cool in summer, and the lively **Bengali Market** (situated on Tansen Marg in central Delhi) where you can taste some of the best Bengali sweets in town at **Nathu's**. Just outside the outer circle, along **Baba Kharak Singh Marg** you will find the **State Emporia Complex** that offers excellent handicrafts from different Indian states. This is the place to buy Kashmiri carpets, shawls and papier-mâché, rather than in the more expensive Kashmir Emporium (in central Delhi). Across the road is a temple to Hanuman, the monkey god. Every Tuesday, a lively market sprawls near the temple where you can find bangles and assorted everyday objects, and have your palms hennaed with traditional designs. To the west of Connaught Place on Mandir Marg, the large, extravagant domes of **Lakshmi Narayan Mandir** (open daily) are hard to miss. This temple to Lakshmi, the goddess of prosperity, is a good introduction to Hindu

---

**HOW TO BUILD A DOME**

Two more palaces were built by Lutyens: **Hyderabad House** for the prince of Hyderabad (then believed to be the richest man in the world), and **Baroda House** for the Maharaja of Baroda. Like Rashtrapati Bhavan, these palaces have domes built without any support in the following ancient Indian tradition: the labourers stood in a circle, brick in hand, while mortar was laid on and music played. At the sound of a drumbeat, they laid their bricks in perfect harmony, thus instantly creating a ring.

**Connaught Place**

temples. Remember to take off your shoes in the reception hall.

Not far from here, in Ashoka Road, is a Sikh temple complex, **Bangla Sahib Gurdwara**, also worth an inspection. Here, beautiful devotional music emanates from the central shrine at all times. Southwest of Connaught Place along Sansad Marg is the surreal pink-and-white **Jantar Mantar**, one of five astrological observatories conceived by Maharaja Jai Singh II – Jaipur's extraordinary ruler in the first half of the 18th century. The sundials can calculate time with astonishing precision. The Jaipur Jantar Mantar is even more impressive and features in the *Guinness Book of Records*. Another place of interest are the **National Rose Garden** (*see* panel on page 44) near the ruins of **Firoz Shah Kotla**. The garden's entrance is Khuni-Darwaza (blood gate – where the British executed two sons of the last emperor), thought to be the surviving gate to **Shergarh**, Sher Shah's city (*see* page 34).

### The Museums

New Delhi has a wealth of museums some of which simply must be seen. The **National Museum** (open Tuesday–Sunday, 10:00–17:00) is easily found just south of the Janpath-Rajpath intersection. It is both large in size and in scope and a great way to learn about the permutations of Indian and Asian aesthetics and cultures. Starting with exhibits dating from 5000 years ago, it traces the evolution of art during different dynasties and eras. Highlights are the **Nagaland masks**, the Buddhist gallery, **carpentry** from Gujarat, the display of 300 musical instruments, the **Central Asian** antiquities and the Indian **miniature gallery** (the largest in the world).

Suitably housed in the former Jaipur House, built by Lutyens for the Maharaja of Jaipur, the **National Gallery of Modern Art** (open daily 10:00–17:00) offers a retrospective view of Indian art over the last 150 years, including work by poet and artist Rabindranath Tagore, the enigmatic folk art inspired Jamini Roy, Ravi Varma's iconographic portraits, and temporary exhibitions by new artists. The popular **Indira Gandhi Memorial Museum** in Safdarjang Road is the tasteful former home of the Gandhi family and contains letters, photos and possessions, including Indira Gandhi's blood-stained sari; part of it is dedicated to her son Rajiv – the clothes he wore when he was assassinated are on display too. The **Nehru Museum** (Teen Murti Marg) up the road is worth a quick look if you are interested in modern Indian history. If, however, you have to choose one museum, that would have to be the **Crafts Museum** (open daily 10:00–17:00) across from the **Purana Qila** (*see* page 50). Here you will find reconstructions of tribal

## THE BELGIAN EMBASSY

One of the most remarkable modern buildings in Delhi, the Belgian embassy is tucked away at the southern end of Shanti Path in the diplomatic enclave of Chanakyapuri. Designed by the world-renowned artist Satish Gujral in the early 1980s, it is a unique and highly conceptual blend of modernized traditional Indian forms, such as the cosmic Hindu configuration of the mandala – the architectural concept of dividing the perfect square into further sequential squares – and it echoes, on a larger scale, Gujral's sculptures.

**Left:** *The National Gallery of Modern Art.*

### THE GREAT BUILDERS

Every new ruler of Hindustan had the ambition to create something bigger and better than his predecessors, which is why Delhi is such an astonishingly multi-layered graveyard of dynasties. Every ruler with a vision left his – and occasionally her – mark. Iltutimish, from the Slave Dynasty, built the Qutab Minar Complex, and Ala-ud-din Khalji from the Khalji Dynasty added the beautiful Alai Darwaza or gatehouse to the mosque in the complex, as well as building his own city, Siri. On a larger scale, Giyas-ud-din Tughluq aspired to create a city that was also a defensive outpost, while his son Mohammed, not content with his father's achievement, erected his own city, Jahanpanah (refuge of the world). The Lodi sultans left extravagant tombs, found in Delhi's Lodi Gardens. The Mughals of course took this trend to yet greater heights, the most striking examples being the extravagant and short-lived Fatehpur Sikri (city of victory) near Agra, Agra Fort and the Red Fort in Delhi. It was not enough to be functional – every new architectural project had to be superlative. The Taj Mahal was built to be the most beautiful tomb in the world and, alongside other Mughal architecture, is a vivid illustration of the Mughals' idealistic concept of creating a 'paradise on earth'.

life in different states of India, set in a village complex complete with an entire wooden *haveli* – a traditional mansion with an interior courtyard (*see* page 43). Master weavers work with beautiful textiles and complex patterns, and there are regular dance, music and puppetry performances, and craft displays and sales.

## Old Delhi

There are many old Delhis, but of all of them, the name refers particularly to the walled city of Shah Jahan, Ruler of the World. The fifth great Mughal emperor was a lover of beautiful architecture. When the construction of the Taj Mahal was underway he turned his attention to the traditional Mughal capital and graced it with a grand new city (Shahjahanabad) and, in 1648, with his royal Peacock Throne. Today almost nothing remains of the city walls and only four of its 14 gates survive – **Kashmiri Gate**, the northern entrance to the walled city, and **Delhi Gate** to the south, followed by **Turkman** and **Ajmeri Gates** to the west. The **Red Fort,** from where the emperor governed Hindustan, is still the architectural highlight of the walled city, together with the biggest mosque in India – **Jama Masjid** (Friday Mosque) – also built by Shah Jahan. Pockets of the past glory of Shahjahanabad can be spotted here and there among the colourful decay and chaotic but good-natured human

**Left:** *The spice market, or Sadar Bazaar, in Old Delhi.*
**Opposite:** *A Kohbarghar wedding chamber in the Crafts Museum.*

and motor traffic of the main thoroughfare **Chandni Chowk** (Moonlight Square). Patience and a spirit of adventure are needed to enjoy this most fascinating and enduring part of Delhi. The hard bargaining at sprawling spice and jewellery markets, the leisurely savouring of Mughal meat dishes at **Karim's** restaurant, the seemingly unchanged medieval back streets of Chandni Chowk where goats and children play in the gutters, the stately, beautifully painted *havelis* tucked away behind arches – all this makes for an unforgettable experience of the immortal capital.

### Red Fort ***

Known as Lal Qila (Red fort) and twice the size of the Agra fort, this mighty palace was Shah Jahan's dream of building 'delightful edifices through which streams of water should flow and the terraces of which should overlook the river'. Though badly damaged in the numerous sackings of Delhi, especially by the British in 1858 when the last emperor was deposed, the fort retains some of its beauty and grandeur. The entrance is through **Lahori Gate** outside which a congregation of rickshaws and vendors accost potential customers. You may be offered the services of a guide. It is better to

---

**THE MARKETS OF OLD DELHI**

**Chawri Bazaar:** located west of Jama Masjid, sells masks, lamps, ashtrays, brass and copper statuettes of Hindu gods.
**Dariba Kalan:** explore the jewellers' street.
**Kinari Bazaar:** sells fine wedding and festival apparel.
**Nai Sarak:** this street running from Chawri Bazaar to Chandni Chowk specializes in beautiful handmade paper and stationery.
**Sadar Bazaar:** past the Fatehpuri Masjid, a wholesale spice market selling the best spices and nuts in Delhi.

**Above:** *The 60-pillared Diwan-i-Am, or Hall of Public Audience.*

---

**ROSES**

The rose was a favourite Mughal flower. Shan Jahan's favourite sweet was rose-flavoured *gulab jamun*. Nur Jahan (Light of the World), the beloved wife of Emperor Jahangir, who was known to ride into battle with him and who built her father the splendid tomb of Itimad-ud-Daulah in Agra, bathed in rose petals. She is thus reputed to have discovered *gulab attar* or rose perfume. Her imposing bath, given to her by Jahangir on their wedding, is in Akbar Mahal in Agra Fort. The **Rose Gardens** near the ruins of Feroz Shah Kotla are lovely in February and March.

---

look for one inside the walls if you don't already have one. Alternatively you may prefer to enjoy this sight at your own leisure. Inside the walls, you will stroll along Chatta Chowk, a bazaar lane that used to service the courtiers with silver, jewels and brocades, and which today offers little more than pre-dictable souvenirs – with the occasional gem. At the beginning of the lane, on the left-hand side and up a staircase, there is a jewellery shop selling interesting if somewhat overpriced silver. The official gateway is **Naqqar-Khana** (drum house) where thunderous music was played to announce the arrival of the emperor. Through the gateway is the red sandstone Hall of Public Audience, **Diwan-i-Am**, where the emperor sat on a raised marble throne to receive his visitors, high and low, and discuss public matters. Executioners stood by, ready to carry out the emperor's sentences. The audience ended with a review of the royal elephants and horses. The pavilion is decorated with *pietra dura* carvings of flowers, birds and a surprising scene of Orpheus with a lute, designed by a Frenchman. The private palaces are beyond the Diwan-i-Am, parallel to the now retreating river. To the far left lie two marble pavilions, the only remains of what used to be the regal, lamp-lit, richly decorated gardens of **Hayat Baksh Bagh** (life-giving gardens). The first significant building to the east is the ethereal **Moti Masjid** or Pearl Mosque, built by Shah Jahan's pious son and usurper of power Aurangzeb for his private prayers. Behind the mosque are the lavishly carved and miraculously preserved mar-ble royal baths or *hammam*. The next building along the marble pavilion of **Diwan-i-Khas**, or Hall of Private

Audience, is the political heart of the complex and aes-
thetically the most beautiful construction. In the centre of
the bejewelled and decorated pavilion stands the
Peacock Throne, pride of the emperor, entirely made of
gold and inlaid with a wealth of precious stones. It was
taken as loot by the Persian Nadir Shah in his bloody
sacking of the capital in the 18th century. At this throne,
the emperor received important visitors and reflected on
matters of state. One of the arches bears an inscription
composed by the famous poet Amir Khusrau: 'If on earth
there be a place of bliss, it is this, it is this, it is this'.

The **Khas Mahal** was the emperor's private quarters,
with separate apartments for prayer, eating and
sleeping. He made public appearances twice a day on his
octagonal balcony before a gathering of citizens down on
the banks of the river. One of the rooms has an exquisite
*jaali* (marble screen) representing the scales of justice.

Conveniently close by is the **Rang Mahal** or Painted
Palace which housed the royal harem. The emperor
would retire here for his lunch to discuss housekeeping

### ARTS AND CRAFTS

In Sanskrit the word *shilpi*
means both artist and craftsman. In India there is no
traditional distinction
between crafts and arts and
this can be appreciated at
the Crafts Museum near the
Purana Qila. Here, over
20,000 showcases of the
best in tribal art are on display. You can watch the
craftsmen in action and
purchase their work. The
master weaver at the
museum creates intricately
embroidered saris which
remain as museum exhibits –
they are truly works of art
and can take up to eight
months to make. There is also
live music and tribal dancing
in the open courtyard.

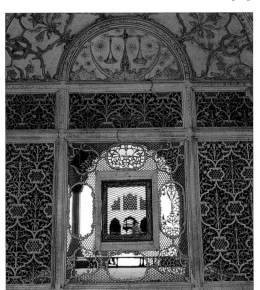

**Left:** *Red Fort, latticed
screen in the Khas Mahal.*

**STEPWELLS AND CHARBAGH**

In Hinduism, stepwells give the daily task of fetching water a spiritual dimension. With the advent of Islam, the concept of *charbagh* or four gardens was introduced, in accordance with which water channels dissecting palace or pavilion grounds were seen as a passage to paradise. This concept is seen in the **Taj Mahal** and its predecessor, **Humayun's Tomb**. The earliest stepwell dates from the seventh century. The height of each landing normally corresponds to an average person's height, so that the water vessel can be transported easily. Stepwells can be seen in the **Nizamuddin** complex and in the **Firoz Shah Kotla** ruins in Delhi, as well as in the Rajasthani countryside.

matters with his favourite daughter Jahanara, first lady since the death of his wife, Mumtaz Mahal. The Palace had a silver ceiling which has since been defaced, and a lotus-shaped marble pool with a silver fountain. The last palace, **Mumtaz Mahal**, is obscure in origin – though it most likely housed some of the harem – and now contains the palace museum. It is worth a quick look.

### Jama Masjid (Friday Mosque) ***

The last of Shah Jahan's great projects was completed two years before he lost his throne to his son Aurangzeb. The Jama Masjid is the largest mosque in India, one of the largest of Islam and it cost one million rupees to build. It is at the heart of Muslim life in Old Delhi, the equivalent of the Nizamuddin village in South Delhi and a spiritual counterpoint to the Red Fort. Its striped minarets and three onion domes dominate Old Delhi and are worth the climb for a breathless panorama of the city. The vast open courtyard with a water tank in the middle for washing before prayer, accommodates up to 20,000 worshippers, though on most days prayers take place inside the main prayer hall to the west (facing

**Left:** *Chandni Chowk, Old Delhi's main arterial road.*
**Opposite:** *The Muslim heart of the Old City – Jama Masjid (Friday Mosque).*

Mecca). Note the striking black marble inlay in the decorations inside and on the domes. The vast sandstone steps leading up to the mosque from three sides are a social hub. Here worshippers read the Qur'an and gossiping men and vendors sell sweet meats and kebabs. You will need to remove your shoes and cover your legs and arms before entering the mosque. Opposite the south entrance is **Karim's restaurant**, a compulsory detour (*see* right panel).

### Chandni Chowk ★★★

You can make your way to the main thoroughfare of Old Delhi either from the **Red Fort**, which is at its eastern end, or from the **Jama Masjid** through the labyrinthine side streets around **Dariba Kalan**. In either case, taking a cycle rickshaw is a more stress-free alternative to walking, which for the first-time visitor, can be overwhelming. Chandni Chowk (Moonlight Square) was constructed by Jahanara, Shah Jahan's favourite daughter. Originally, there was an octagonal pool in front of the Lahori Gate of the Red Fort, into which a branch of the Stream of Paradise – a watering system in the palace – flowed creating a beautiful effect in the moonlight and

---

**THE TWO KARIMS**

The original Karim is in Matia Mahal, a lane south of the Jama Masjid, the other at the heart of Nizamuddin village. The two restaurants are run by the successors of the original owners who were chefs at the Mughal court. The idea was to bring royal cuisine to the people. The one in Matia Mahal has five dining halls and offers great hands-on displays of Muslim cooking in the internal courtyard: brews in huge pots and various methods of making *roti* and *naan*. There is a variety of excellent kebabs and very good vegetarian dishes. The family recipes are a secret not revealed even to the staff in the kitchen: the women in the family make the elaborate spice mixture themselves, as well as Karim's special *khir* (rice and milk pudding in earthenware). A favourite is the *badam pasanda*, almond and curd lamb. No alcohol is available.

giving the avenue its name. It was lined with trees and water channels among which the liveliest commerce in the East took place. If your starting point is the Red Fort, the first sight of interest, straight to your left, is the **Jain Temple**, which also doubles as a **bird hospital**. The temple dates from the 16th century and has some gilded ornamentation and carvings. In its courtyard is the bird hospital, housing sick birds in tune with the Jain principle of preserving all life. Regular patients here are partridges wounded in the partridge fights that are among Old Delhi-*wallahs*' (residents) favourite pastimes. Further down Chandni Chowk is the large **Gurdwara Sisganj**, a Sikh temple dedicated to a guru beheaded by Emperor Aurangzeb. Here, he also displayed the beheaded corpse of his learned and liberal brother Dara Shukoh, favourite son of Shah Jahan.

**Opposite:** *Site of Mahatma Gandhi's cremation, now a public park.*

Just around the corner from the Gurdwara is **Dariba Kalan** the jewellers' street, where you can find exceptional new and antique silverware at low prices. To the left is **Kinari Bazaar**, a glittering market lane selling wedding and festival apparel including saris, masks of Hindu deities and swords. Every object here shines with gold or silver tinsel. At the corner of Dariba Kalan and Chandni Chowk you can make a quick stop at the popular sweet shop of Naim Chand Jain, selling *jalebi* twirls (fried treacle tubes soaked in hot syrup), similar in sweetness to *gulab jamun*. Further down and across Chandni Chowk is the British-built **Town Hall** (1860s) behind which lies the peaceful **Mahatma Gandhi Park**, once built as the Queen's Gardens and today a favourite haunt for *sadhus* (Hindu ascetics). Towards the west end of the avenue is **Fatehpuri Mosque**, financed by Begum Fatehpuri, one of Shah Jahan's wives. Outside the mosque begin stalls selling nuts and dried fruit which gradually blend into spice stalls – a sign that the intense **spice market** or **Sadar Bazaar** is approaching. It is tucked away behind a gateway, so ask for directions. You will find every imaginable spice here, if you have the nerve to sneeze your way through the noisy throngs!

## Memorial Ghats

Wherever there is a river in India, there are *ghats* or river steps – for washing, fetching water, bathing, and executing cremations. Along the bank of the Yamuna, right of

### SHOPPING

Only Jaipur beats Delhi as shoppers' cheap paradise, but Delhi is better for its indoor emporia and fixed-price shopping. Credit cards are accepted in most of the recommended places. The **State Emporia Complex** just outside the outer circle of Connaught Place has excellent handicrafts from different Indian states and is the best outlet of this type. Here is the place to buy Kashmiri carpets, shawls and papier-mâché. The more expensive **Kashmir Emporium** (block B, Connaught Place) has the best Kashmiri merchandise. For a similarly orderly selection of the best Indian handicrafts, handlooms and good service go to the two-storey **Central Cottage Industries Emporium**, corner of **Janpath** and **Tolstoy Marg**. For browsers, the **Tibetan** market along **Janpath** has Tibetan jewellery, knick-knacks and junk, while the **Janpath market** (in a lane off Janpath) has exquisite, authentic Rajasthani textiles sold by a row of hard-bargaining tribal women. For the upmarket boutique shopper, stylish **Santoshti Shopping Centre** in Chanakyapuri (next to Samrat Hotel) and **Hauz Khas village** are a must. For art and antiques Hauz Khas village and **Sundar Nagar** (near Purana Qila) are the best.

Mahatma Gandhi Road, there are several *ghats* that are also memorials to Indian politicians. **Raj Ghat** at the south end is where Mahatma Gandhi was cremated in 1948. There is now a moving memorial on the spot. Nearby is the **Gandhi Memorial Museum**, celebrating the life and ideas of the Mahatma. Further up the river is **Shanti Vana** (Forest of Peace) where the first prime minister of India, Jawaharlal Nehru, as well as his daughter Indira Gandhi and her two sons Sanjay and Rajiv were cremated. **Vijay Ghat** is dedicated to India's second prime minister, Lal Bahadur Shastri.

## SOUTH DELHI

South of Lutyens's Delhi is where you will find traces of some of the **old cities** merging with fashionable complexes like **Hauz Khas**, and the fascinating medieval Muslim enclave of **Nizamuddin**.

### Purana Qila and Sundar Nagar

East of India Gate and between Mathura and Outer Ring Road lie the splendid ruins of Purana Qila – today the scene of theatrical and musical performances. At this multi-layered site, centuries of dreams and fates of different rulers overlap. The earliest traces here are from the legendary city of **Indraprastha**, which features in the

**Below:** *The Old Fort, Purana Qila, built by the Afghan Sher Shah.*

*Mahabharata*. But what still stands today are the remnants of **Shergarh**, the sixth city of Delhi built by the Afghan ruler Sher Shah. Having moved from Agra to Delhi, the Mughal emperor Humayun dreamt of ruling from his new city **Dinpanah** (Shelter of Faith) when Sher Shah invaded and forced him into exile.

He expanded the city of Humayun northwards and called it Shergarh. The entrance gate stands by Firoz Shah Kotla and two of the principle buildings of Purana Qila survive: Qal'a-i-Kuhna-Masjid (Old Fort Mosque) consisting of five arches made of marble-inlaid sandstone, and Sher Mandal where Humayun fell to his death (*see* right panel). You can ascend the stairs on which he stumbled, and enjoy a panoramic view of Delhi and the Yamuna River. Making your way south to **Humayun's Tomb**, you will pass through **Sundar Nagar** market where a number of excellent shops sell antique jewellery and art for the connoisseur.

## Humayun's Tomb

Although Emperor Humayun spent 15 years in exile while Sher Shah occupied Delhi, his reign marks the beginning of the Mughal golden era. A learned and refined man, he died in a fall from the top of his library after he had returned to reclaim the seat of power. His wife Bega (Haji) Begum undertook the construction of a splendid tomb which became a landmark in an epoch of great Mughal architecture, reaching its apogee in the **Taj Mahal**. Its Persian architect used the Qur'anic concept of Paradise in a garden setting. The quadrangle divisions of

**Above:** *Humayun's Tomb, the predecessor of the Taj Mahal.*

### HUMAYUN'S DEATH

Emperor Humayun was exiled to Persia after Afghan Emperor Sher Shah invaded Delhi and created the city of **Shergarh** at the site of ancient city **Purana Qila**. Only two of the fort buildings survive today, including the octagonal Sher Mandal which Humayun, on his return to Delhi, made into his library. It was here, at the top of the stairs, that he stood one night looking out for the transit of Venus, tripped over his robes and plummeted to his death. His tomb, the first great Mughal tomb, was built by his widow Bega Begum who is also buried there.

its grounds, introducing the *charbagh* (four-garden) idea, is seen on a larger scale in the Taj Mahal. Mughals entombed here are Dara Shukoh (favourite son of Shah Jahan, who was murdered by his brother Auranzgeb), emperors Farrukhsiyar and Alamgir – both murdered, and Bega Begum, the tomb's creator. Open daily.

### Lodi Gardens

Named after the Lodi Sultan dynasty which ruled Delhi from the mid-15th century to the 1520s, the garden grounds today contain several tombs of Lodi and Sayyid sultans (the dynasty before the Lodis). Best to visit at dusk when the tombs are lit up and the park is quietly overrun with joggers.

### Safdarjang's Tomb

In contrast to Humayun's mausoleum, this tomb was built in the last throes of Mughal power and marks the end of this golden age. Safdarjang was an influential and progressive minister to the Emperor Ahmad Shah in the mid-18th century. The emperor himself, described as 'a vicious, dissipated, perfidious, pusillanimous and utterly worthless young man', was eventually duly deposed. Safdarjang's son spent 300,000 rupees on his father's tomb, marking the last and decadent phase of Mughal architecture. The rooftop views are worth a climb.

### Nizamuddin ★★★

Nizamuddin, named after a 13th-century Muslim prophet, is a prosperous residential area at whose heart lies a village dating from medieval times. It is accessible

---

**QAWWALI**

*Qawwali* is a devotional music form practised by the Sufi Muslims of India and Pakistan. Today's *qawwals* (exclusively male singers) claim descent from the poet Amir Khusrau, during whose anniversary the singing goes on day and night. The chief mystic associated with this music is Hizrat Nizamuddin and *qawwali* can be heard most reliably in his shrine in Nizamuddin village, especially at festival times. The chanting, accompanied by *tabla* (hand drums) and harmonium, is incantatory and known to induce hypnotic states, associated with spiritual ecstasy in listeners. Despite its religious nature, *qawwali* is also hugely popular and some of its top performers have recorded CDs and achieved star status.

from the south via **Mathura Road**. Stroll along its busy, narrow lanes passing through great wooden gates, and savour the Muslim way of life with its kebab aromas and the distant sound of Sufi religious chanting or *qawwali*. For women, it is imperative to cover legs, arms and heads, especially as you near the *dargah* or shrine of the saint. Entering the shrine area, you pass stalls selling rose petals, Islamic books, CDs of *qawwali*, incense and other indispensables for the visit to Nizamuddin's tomb. Before entering the shrine complex you must leave your shoes with a shoe keeper who will give you a token in exchange for a few rupees. You could be approached by smart men asking you to 'sign the book', i.e. give a donation.

The ascetic Hazrat Nizamuddin lived here for 90 years and had a large following. Belonging to the Chishti order of Sufis, he believed that spiritual ecstasy could be reached through music. To this day, some 200 families related to Nizamuddin and his disciples live from donations to the shrine. Surrounding Nizamuddin's shrine are the smaller tombs of some of his noted disciples: the poet Amir Khusrau, whose poetry set to music is still heard here, especially during the celebration of his anniversary in April when the *qawwali* continues throiughout the night, as well as the mighty Mughal emperor Muhammed Shah and Jahanara, Shah Jahan's favourite daughter whose tomb is filled with earth, in accordance with her wish to have nothing but grass cover her grave. A large sandstone mosque to the left, the oldest building

**Opposite:** *The imposing Bara Gumbal Tomb located in Lodi Gardens.* **Below** *Nizamuddin's Tomb at the heart of Nizamuddin Village.*

in the area, dates from 1325 and is actively in use at least five times a day. You may exit through the northern gate on the other side of the tomb, where you will find a step-well with holy water, built by Ghiyasuddin Tughlaq (who also built the **Tughluqabad Fort**).

### Hauz Khas ★★★

Midway between Safdarjang and the Qutab Minar, Hauz Khas village is a cluster of elegant designer boutiques, antique shops and restaurants flanked by the remains of Delhi's second city Siri and a deer park. The pleasant relaxed atmosphere of the shopping lanes leads you into shops stocked with a variety of Indian crafts and designs – from furniture and lampshades to high quality jewellery and clothing. There are also some galleries where you can purchase contemporary Indian art. Upon reaching the end of the main street you will come face to face with the remains of the great water reservoir or *hauz* and its adjacent ruins of a university, built at a later stage by Firoz Shah, as well as a number of tombs that include the humble one of Firoz Shah himself. The ancient grounds are popular with picnickers. At night the ruins are lit up and a number of stylish rooftop restaurants in the village complex offer a magical view and good food.

---

**THE CURSE OF NIZAMUDDIN**

When the first of the Tughluq dynasty of Sultans, Ghiyas-ud-din Tughluq, began the construction of his new city – now the third city of Delhi – he allegedly refused to build a Sufi shrine. Thereupon the Sufi saint Nizamuddin prophesied that the new citadel would remain uninhabited. This curse was fulfilled when the Sultan died in a freak accident and his son, Mohammed, abandoned the city due to a water short-age. Today, Tughluqabad is the most melancholy of Delhi's seven cites. Walking over its ruins, the look over the aggressive new suburban sprawl across the plain is a powerful reminder of the continuous rise and fall of powerful empires.

## Baha'i Temple

Shaped like a giant lotus flower and made from white Rajasthani marble, the Baha'i Temple dominates the Kalkaji area in the southeast of the city. It is somewhat reminiscent of the Sydney Opera House in its modernist boldness. Its central hall reaches 34m (112 feet). To the south, the contrasting **Kalkaji Temple** – dedicated to the blood-thirsty Hindu goddess Kali – is a testimony to the endurance of tradition and ancient faiths.

## Qutab Minar Complex

In the 8th century, the Tomara Rajput clan built the citadel of **Lal Kot**. Four centuries later another Rajput clan took over and renamed the city **Qila Rai Pithora**, the first city of Delhi. Most of this ancient site was destroyed by the invading Afghan armies who established the **Delhi Sultanate** that marked the beginning of a long Muslim rule over Northern India. Many Hindu temples were destroyed and their intricately carved stones used to build the first Islamic monument of India – **Quwwat-ul-Islam Masjid** (Might of Islam Mosque). The first Muslim ruler, **Qutab-ud-din-Aibak** (*see* page 10), wasted no time and embarked on the construction of the mosque surrounding an ancient iron pillar. The majestic **Qutab Minar**, a 73m (238 feet) minaret in red sandstone and the most enduring landmark of Delhi, was thought to have been built by Aibak's successor and son-in-law, Iltutmish. It is intricately carved and inscribed with excerpts from the Qur'an. However, recent research shows that all the Medieval Muslims did was put a fancy new coat on a tower built nearly 2000 years previously as a giant sundial.

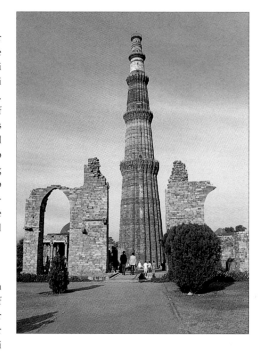

**Above:** *The majestic Qutab Minar, the oldest landmark of Delhi.*
**Opposite:** *The lotus-shaped Baha'i Temple.*

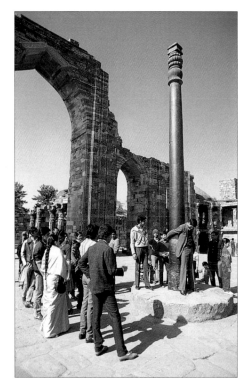

In the 14th century, Emperor Feroz Shah undertook some repairs of the minaret, adding two storeys in marble and a cupola that was replaced by the British, but later mocked and removed; today it stands on the lawns as a canopy. Unfortunately, access to the inside staircase that leads up to the superb balconies has been closed due to suicides and accidents. A gatehouse (**Alai Darwaza**) to the mosque was built by another ruler. This graceful yet solid structure made from red sandstone and white marble has intricate carvings and lotus-bud motifs, all elements which were to reappear in countless Indian buildings in the centuries to come. After touring the complex, an English bishop observed that 'they built like giants, and they finished like jewellers'. Next to the gate, inside the mosque

**Above:** *People used to grasp the Iron Pillar at Qutab Minar Complex in order to make their wishes come true.*

**Opposite:** *Tughluqabad Fort, once the powerful seat of the first Tughluq Sultan.*

courtyard, stands the mysterious **Iron Pillar**, the single non-Islamic structure in the complex. It bears Sanskrit inscriptions and dates from the 4th century Gupta period. Its origins are unknown, as is the technique used to ensure that the pure iron has remained totally rust-free. Legend has it that whoever manages to encircle the pillar with their arms will have their wish fulfilled. With the pillar now fenced off, the wishes have to wait.

About 1km (0.6 miles) to the west is **Mehrauli village**. The detour is worth making for the boutiques, the good Italian café, and the smattering of ruins and tombs in the area. Most noted is the octagonal tomb of Adham Khan, also known as Bhul-Bhulaiyan (labyrinth) for its intricate passages. This general and foster brother of emperor

Akbar was repeatedly thrown from the walls of Agra fort (on the order of the emperor) after murdering the imperial chief minister. His tomb was built at Akbar's order.

## Tughluqabad

8km (5 miles) east of Qutab Minar stand the remains of the **third city of Delhi**, built by Ghiyas-ud-din Tughluq, the first of the Tughluq sultans who reigned from the early 14th- to the early 15th century. The city consisted of three parts: the massive fort (near the entrance today) with 13 gates, the palaces to the left of the citadel, and to the north the grid-planned city of which some streets can still be traced. Today, only a tower and some subterranean passages remain, and the ruins are haunted by rhesus monkeys and nomads. It is believed that when the new citadel was built, the saint Nizamuddin predicted it was soon to be abandoned and inhabited only by Gujar robbers (*see* page 54). The sultan intended to punish him but met an untimely death. His eccentric son Mohammed took over, but had to leave Tughluqabad only five years after its completion due to a lack of fresh water. He moved 1500km (930 miles) southwards with his people, only to return and found the fourth city of Delhi, **Jahanpanah**, north of the Qutab Minar (not much remains of it today). The impressive mausoleum of Ghyias-ud-din, made from red sandstone and marble, contains the remains of the sultan, his wife and their son.

**NEEMRANA FORT PALACE-HOTEL**

On the main highway from Delhi to Jaipur, about 120km (76 miles) from Delhi, there is a magical Rajasthani hilltop fort-palace. It was built in the mid-15th century by one Raja Rajdeo, who had fled from the aftermath of the Muslim invasions. An Indian art historian and a Frenchman converted it into a stunningly atmospheric hotel, with great taste and attention to detail. Decorated with hand-printed textiles and antique doors and furniture, this is India's oldest heritage hotel and a worthwhile detour on the way to Jaipur or back to Delhi. On weekends, visitors from Delhi flock here. The hotel also offers a buffet breakfast on the rooftop veranda and fabulous character 'loos with a view'. Tel: (01494) 246 0068, website: www. neemranahotels.com

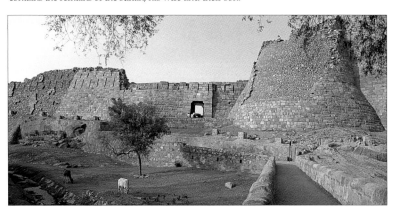

# Delhi at a Glance

## BEST TIMES TO VISIT

The **coolest** time to visit Delhi is between October and February. **March** and **April** get warm, reaching scorching temperatures in **May** and **June** – often accompanied by dust storms. The **monsoon** season usually starts around **July** and is best avoided because it also brings mosquitoes. **September** is humid and muggy, with temperatures in the 30s, but it can still be pleasant. **October** and **November** are the best months to visit.

## GETTING THERE

**Indira Gandhi International Airport**, tel: (011) 2565 2021 (international), (011) 2567 5181 (domestic) is a 30-minute drive southwest of the city centre. Book a hotel room at the reservations desk in the departure hall. Taxi rates for airport transfers are normally fixed, with a surcharge at night. There are two main railway stations – **New Delhi Station** and **Delhi Station** in Old Delhi. Railway bookings: International Tourist Bureau, 1st Floor, New Delhi Station, tel: 1330/35/45; website: www.indianrail.gov.in There are flights and trains to both Agra and Jaipur. Air India, tel: (011) 2373 8004; British Airways, tel: (011) 2331 6611; Virgin Atlantic, tel: (011) 5150 1300/05; Etihad, tel: (011) 3901 3901; Jet Air, tel: 091-5164 1414/3636; Indian Airlines, tel: 011-2462 0566/2220.

## GETTING AROUND

Take a **taxi** for longer distances – including to and from the airport. Negotiate the fare first or use a set-rate taxi from the DTTDC (see page 59). There are taxi stands in Connaught Place and around in New Delhi. In New Delhi **auto-rickshaws** are a good and cheap alternative to the taxi. In Old Delhi and for smaller stretches, **cycle-rickshaws** are safe. Delhi now has its first metro line, currently looping across the north of the Old City and not terribly useful to travellers, but construction on the next line is well under way and that will link up with Connaught Place. Fares are cheap, the system is fast and best of all, it will help keep traffic off the overcongested roads. As every journey involves haggling, it is worth hiring a taxi or auto-rickshaw by the day.

## WHERE TO STAY

### *LUXURY*

**ITC Maurya Sheraton**, Diplomatic Enclave, tel: (011) 2611 2233; fax: (011) 2611 3333; www.welcomgroup.com Three wings, a special floor for women travellers, a pool and health club, shopping centre and some fine restaurants, including Bukhara, specializing in northwest frontier cuisine, and Dum Phukt, imperial cuisine unlike any other Indian food.
**Imperial**, Janpath, tel: (011) 2334 1234, fax: (011) 2334 2255; www.theimperialindia.com

Established hotel from the 30s, with authentic Raj ambience and a recent overhaul. Great location, outdoor bar, breakfast buffet and a fine Asian restaurant – the Thai Spice Route.
**Taj Mahal**, 1 Man Singh Road, tel: (011) 2302 6162, fax: (011) 2302 6070; www.tajhotels.com Splendid Raj-style ambience, highly ornate. Has one of the best French restaurants in Delhi, Longchamp; an excellent Indian *Mughlai* restaurant, Haveli, with live music; and the exceptional Chinese House of Ming.
**Uppals Orchid**, National Highway 8, near airport, tel: (011) 2506 1515; fax: (011) 2506 1516; www. uppalsorchidhotel.com Resort set in lush gardens and park. An eco-hotel, they do take the label seriously, from using recycled timber in building to using decorations other than cut flowers. Nine-hole golf course and pool.

### *UPMARKET TO MID-RANGE*

**Ambassador**, Sujan Singh Park (near India Gate), tel: (011) 2463 2600, fax: (011) 2463 2252; www.tajhotels.com Large, comfortable rooms, disco and one of the best South Indian restaurants.
**Claridges**, 12 Aurangzeb Road, tel: (011) 2301 0211, fax: (011) 2301 0625; e-mail: claridges.hotel@ gems.vsnl.net.in Old-fashioned, stylish, with pool and a touch of decadence.

# Delhi at a Glance

Restaurants include Dhaba (Indian), Jade Garden (Chinese) and Pickwick (Continental). Outdoor restaurant and bar. **Broadway**, Asaf Ali Road, tel: (011) 2327 3821. Just west of Delhi Gate, Chor Bizarre – top restaurant of Old Delhi, views over Jama Masjid.

*BUDGET*
**Ahuja Residency**, 193 Golf Links, tel: (011) 2461 1027; www.ahujaresidency.com Delightful guesthouse in a 50s mansion near Khan Market. Rooms vary in size and style. Book ahead.
**Master Paying Guest Accommodation**, R-500 New Rajinder Nagar, tel: (011) 2574 1089; www.master-guesthouse.com Small (only 4 rooms) guesthouse carefully designed and run along spiritual principles; roof terrace, reiki treatments.
**Nirula's**, L-block, Connaught Place, tel: (011) 2332 2419, fax: (011) 2335 3957; www.nirulas.com Air-conditioning, good lively restaurants. Not the cheapest.
**Palace Heights**, D-block, Connaught Place, tel: (011) 332 1419. Nice but small rooms, some air conditioned. Terrace, Internet café, reasonably priced.

WHERE TO EAT
Most of the best restaurants are in the hotels. Check out the stunning Thai Blue Elephant and Baluchi (Northern Indian) at the Hotel InterContinental in Barakhamba Road; the sublime,

low-priced South Indian Coconut Grove in Ashok Yatri Niwas, 19 Ashoka Rd, tel: (011) 334 4511, and Le Belvedere and Pierre, two fine French restaurants at Le Meridien, Windsor Place, Janpath, tel: (011) 2371 0101. In town, Connaught Place has a wide selection (see panel, page 38).
**Dilli Haat**, opp. INA Market. The best place to wander along munching fresh snacks from across India. Cheap and cheerful, with great atmosphere.
**The Big Chill Café**, 68a Khan Market, tel: (011) 5175 7588. Trendy Western café; salads, pasta, cakes and ice creams.
**Karim's**, see panel, page 47.
**Pindi**, 16 Pandara Road Market, tel: (011) 2338 7932. Pleasant, friendly *dhaba* restaurant, with air-conditioning and affordable north Indian food.
**Turquoise Cottage**, 81/3 Adhchiui, Sti Aurobindo Marg, tel: (011) 2696 3234. Smart Thai/Chinese restaurant near the Qutab Minar; dim sum and barbecue, with a trendy bar.
**Village Bistro Complex**, Hauz Khas village. Top Indian cuisine, outdoor dining with view of South Delhi. The village also has other fine restaurants.

TOURS AND EXCURSIONS
Tours of Delhi are organized through your hotel or the offices below. **Government of India Tourist Office**, 88 Janpath, tel: (011) 2332 0008; www.tourismofindia.com
**Delhi Tourism & Transport Development Corporation** (**DTTDC**), N-36 Connaught Place, tel: (011) 2331 5322; www.delhitourism.nic.in
**Central Reservations Office**, Coffee House I, Baba Kharak Singh Road, opp. Hanuman Temple; tel: (011) 2336 3607/5358. Counters at the two main railway stations and at the International Airport.

USEFUL CONTACTS
**All-India Institute of Medical Sciences**, Ansari Nagar, Sri Aurobindo Marg, tel: (011) 2656 1123. Open 24 hours.
**Thomas Cook**, Hotel Imperial, Janpath; tel: (011) 2334 2171.
**American Express**, A-Block Connaught Place; tel: (011) 2371 9506.
There are many ATM machines and internet cafés, particularly around Connaught Place. *First City*, *The Delhi City*, *City Info* and *Star Delhi Online* are all good listings magazines.

| DELHI | J | F | M | A | M | J | J | A | S | O | N | D |
|---|---|---|---|---|---|---|---|---|---|---|---|---|
| AVERAGE TEMP. °C | 14 | 17 | 23 | 29 | 34 | 35 | 31 | 30 | 30 | 27 | 21 | 16 |
| AVERAGE TEMP. °F | 57 | 63 | 73 | 84 | 93 | 95 | 88 | 86 | 86 | 81 | 70 | 61 |
| HOURS SUN DAILY | 11 | 12 | 12 | 12 | 14 | 14 | 14 | 14 | 13 | 12 | 12 | 11 |
| RAINFALL mm | 25 | 22 | 17 | 7 | 8 | 65 | 211 | 173 | 150 | 31 | 1 | 5 |
| RAINFALL in | 1 | 0.9 | 0.7 | 0.3 | 0.3 | 2.5 | 8.2 | 6.8 | 5.9 | 1.2 | 0.04 | 0.2 |

# 3
# Jaipur

Jaipur is the capital of **Rajasthan** – one of India's most fascinating, historical and colourful states. This gateway to the vast **Thar Desert** was once the seat of the fierce and independent Rajput rulers; enduring showcase of the rigidity of the caste system; and today a bustling, surreal city of 2.5 million where slums coexist with opulent palaces. This is also the most visited part of India, after Agra. Until independence in 1947 this was a self-contained kingdom known as **Rajputana** or Land of Kings, consisting of as many as 22 states ruled for centuries by the Rajputs or princes. The most remarkable of these were the **Kachhawaha Rajputs**, a warrior clan whose arrival to these parts is traced back to the 12th century. At first denied power due to alleged low birth, they successfully established themselves, claiming descent from the sun and moon. They performed ritual cleansing through fire and lived by a strict and bloody code of honour which was applied not only when dealing with invaders – such as the Muslims – but also among their own families. The Rajputs placed themselves in a caste above all others and proceeded to rule Rajputana with considerable efficiency for the next six centuries from their capital **Amber**. They heroically fought off the onslaughts of the sultans of Delhi. When the Mughals came into power, it was the great emperor **Akbar** who first induced the Rajputs to cooperate with the new rulers by marrying a Kachhawaha princess. This augmented the prosperity of Rajputana and created an unprecedented united Hindustan.

---

**DON'T MISS**

**\*\*\* Hawa Mahal:** see the ornate façade of the 'Palace of Winds'.
**\*\*\* Jaipur City Palace:** in the heart of the old city, now part of the Maharajah Sawai Man Singh II Museum.
**\*\*\* Jantar Mantar Observatory:** built by Sawai Jai Singh II in the 18th century.
**\*\*\* Bazaars:** explore the many colourful street stalls.
**\*\*\* Ram Niwas Gardens:** housing the magnificent Albert Hall and an old zoo.

---

**Opposite:** *A bright-eyed little girl dressed for a street wedding in Jaipur.*

**ONE AND A QUARTER**

Jai Singh was crowned ruler of Amber at the age of 12. When he was 15 the Mughal emperor Aurangzeb tried to remove him by sending him to fight against a tribe further south. When he refused, he was brought before the emperor. Aurangzeb enquired how the young king intended to protect his kingdom and life. Jai Singh answered that he expected the emperor himself to protect him, just as a groom would protect his bride. The emperor was so impressed by his wit that he called him *Sawai* (one and a quarter), a title that was passed on to all Kachhawaha rulers from then on. A flag and a quarter of a flag was flown above the palaces of Jaipur as a reminder to other rulers.

In the 18th century, the most talented and visionary of Rajputs, **Jai Singh II**, built the new capital of Jaipur calling it after himself. He had been crowned ruler of Amber at the tender age of 12, after the death of his father. The first three or so decades of his rule were spent consolidating his power through active service to the Mughals and his kingdom, winning substantial military, diplomatic and financial success. Finally, on the laurels of a brilliant career, at the age of 38, he was able to rest and dedicate himself to his favourite pastimes: art and science. With the immense fortune he had amassed, and with the help of gifted Bengali architect **Vidyadhar Bhattacharaya**, he embarked on a grandiose project, the first of its kind in northern India – building a city from scratch.

## THE PINK CITY

Jaipur has remained virtually unchanged from its original plan. It is as vibrant and commercially alive now as it was in the time of Jai Singh II. The construction took only seven years, by which time a glorious **City Palace** was built, as well as temples, markets, *haveli* (townhouses for the aristocracy), residential districts and the extraordinary **Jantar Mantar** is the largest stone observatory in the world – all still in place today. The fantastic **Hawa Mahal** or Palace of Winds was built later that century by another maharaja for his harem. The characteristic **pink** colour of the buildings was a later addition: it was applied to the central district in 1856 as a gesture of welcome on the occasion of the visit of British Prince Albert and it has remained so ever since. Municipal regulations require each homeowner to repaint their façade regularly in order to maintain the appealing pink look of the city. Although many sights of interest are within the Pink City, modern Jaipur comprises more than Jai Singh's walled city. Raj palaces are scattered all around, as are slums – one third of the population live without sewage. The combination of

**Opposite:** *View of the Pink City from the breathtaking Hawa Mahal, or Palace of Winds.*

The sacred Hindu scriptures,
the *Vedas*, conceived of a
Cosmic Man whose body
could be seen as an abstract
numerical system on the
basis of which the material
world could be constructed.
The buildings in Jaipur are
designed to reflect this principle. The *Vasta Purusha
Mandala* is a mathematical
concept based on the *Vedas*,
where the *mandala* is the
perfect square divided into
further sequential squares
of 1, 4, 9, 16, 25, 36, 49,
81 and up to 1024. This
scheme, when implemented
in town planning, is rigidly
hierarchical. Each segment of
the *mandala* is reserved for a
particular caste: *brahmins* in
the north, *kshatriyas* (or
Rajputs) in the east, *vaishyas*
(merchants) in the south,
*shudras* (servants) in the
west, with separate districts
housing different trades.

**pollution** and **heat** in the summer is unbearable, so try
to stay out of peak-hour traffic and have insect repellant
to protect you from mosquitoes.

The design of the city followed a prescribed text on
Hindu architecture – *Shilpa Shastra* – according to which
all different parts should be contained within a grid-
structure or *mandala*, encompassing blocks (seven in this
case) divided by avenues. This is evident on street maps
that depict the grid within the city walls, while modern
Jaipur follows a random plan. Ten wall-gates survive
today, contributing to the enchanting atmosphere of the
pink city. The hectically busy **Badi Chaupar** crossroads
is the heart of the commercial district, next to the Hawa
Mahal. It lies in the middle of the main artery stretching
from **Suraj Pol** (Sun Gate) in the east to **Chand Pol**
(Moon Gate) in the west. Each block was designed to
house a particular craft or activity – hence Suraj Pol
Bazaar is the elephant owners' quarters, **Johari Bazaar** is
a market for jewellery and cotton fabrics, **Bapu** and
**Nehru Bazaars** for textiles, shoes and perfumes.

The three most important landmarks lie within
the **City Palace complex** which forms the core of the
beautiful Pink City.

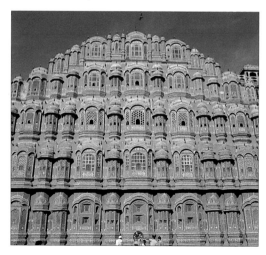

**Opposite:** *Magnificent
Jaipur City Palace.*
**Right:** *Hawa Mahal with
its 953 latticed windows.*

### Hawa Mahal ★★★

Unmissable and bizarre with its pink, highly ornamental decor-like appearance, the Hawa Mahal or Palace of Winds is not, and never was, much more than a splendid façade. Built in the last year of the 18th century by the poet-maharaja Sawai Pratap Singh for his wives, courtesans and their attendants, its purpose was to enable the women to observe city life and processions while remaining unseen in *purdah* (behind a veil). The five-storey sandstone building has 953 latticed windows and balconies constructed in such a way that the slightest breeze would cool the observers they concealed. Climbing the stairs you will realize that the edifice is only a room deep and has no solid back wall. Moreover, the top floor offers great views of the colourful, buzzing city streets below. Open 09:00–16:30 daily.

### Jaipur City Palace ★★★

The royal family still live in a portion of the **Chandra Mahal** (Moon Palace) – though most of it, known as the City Palace Museum, has been open to the public since 1959. Visitors enter through the **Atish Pol**

Jaipur City Palace

KEY
1. Pritam Niwas Chowk (Hall of the Beloved)
2. Ridhi Sidhi Pol (Peacock Gate)
3. Diwan-i-Khas (Hall of Private Audience)
4. Sarbato Bhadra Chowk
5. Carriage Museum
6. Sarhad ki Deorhi/Singh Pol (Lion Gate)
7. Chandni Chowk
8. Atish Pol (Stable Gate)
9. Tripolia Gate
10. Gainda Ka Deorhi (Main Entrance)
11. Naqqar Darwaza
12. Sire Deorhi Gate

(Stable Gate) or **Gainda Ka Deorhi**, if travelling from Hawa Mahal, while **Tripolia** (Three-arched) **Gate** is reserved for the royals. The first building you come across is the marble-and-sandstone **Mubarak Mahal** (Palace of Welcome) which was built by Madho Singh II (son of Jai Singh II) to receive foreign visitors. It is now a textile museum displaying the finest royal outfits in silk, muslin and cotton, embroidered coats, *pashmina* shawls and block-printed fabrics. The star of the collection is the pink, padded *atamsikh* (soul delighter) or quilted robe of Madho Singh I who stood 2.1m (7 feet) tall and weighed 225kg (500 pounds). There are also musical instruments and the toys of the princes and princesses, Jaipur blue pottery and Mughal glass. The building in the corner houses the impressive **Sileh Khana** (royal Rajput armoury), a collection of beautiful daggers, swords, spears and body armour inlaid with ivory, jade, silver and gold. There are also inscribed swords that belonged to Shah Jahan and Man Singh I, a Persian imperial sword and the turban-helmet worn by Jai Singh I in battle.

The stunning, marble-inlaid **Sarhad ki Deorhi**, also called Singh Pol (Lion Gate), was decorated with elephants carved out of a single piece of marble on the occasion of the current maharaja's birth in 1931. Through the brass-plated gates you enter the courtyard of the **Diwan-i-Khas** (Hall of Private Audience). Note the continuation of the Mughal trend of having separate buildings for different activities. Under its pink arches stand the two largest silver objects in the world, the vessels were made from 243kg (536 pounds) of silver and can hold up to 1182 litres (2080 pints). When Madho Singh II embarked on a voyage to England in 1901 to attend the coronation of King Edward VII, he chartered an ocean liner, built a temple on board, and set sail

## THE EXTRAVAGANCE OF THE RAJPUTS

The Rajputs, or Princes of Rajputana, never did anything in half measure. Their code of honour was rigid and extreme (it included practices such as self-immolation and blood feuds) and was what made them such outstanding warriors. Their architecture is often dream-like and fantastic, but also enduring and grand, as seen in the Jaipur City Palace, Amber Palace, the Hawa Mahal, the unique Jantar Mantar observatory and Rambagh Palace, and in Rajasthani palaces such as Gwalior Fort and Datia Palace (see pages 118–120). Rajput extravagance also manifested itself in parades and celebrations when the extraordinary wealth of the maharajas was put on display through elephants, jewellery, gold, and, in the 20th century, luxury cars. When Madho Singh II embarked on a voyage to England for the coronation of Edward VII, he threw bags of gold, silver and silk into Bombay harbour for propitious winds. Today, a glimpse of this glorious past can be seen at the Elephant Festival in Jaipur.

throwing bags of gold, silver and silk into Mumbai harbour for good luck. He carried along these specially made silver vessels full of Ganges drinking water to avoid contamination from 'impure' foreign water.

To the right stands the **Diwan-i-Am**, formerly Hall of Public Audience, now the Palace Art Gallery. The painted walls are hung with lush and rare Mughal carpets from Agra, Lahore and other places. Exhibits of interest include gold and silver thrones, glass chandeliers and miniatures from the Jaipur school (attended by Jai Singh II) and from the Mughal school. Passing through the Diwan-i-Khas courtyard again and through a small marble gateway in its left corner called **Ridhi Sidhi Pol**, you reach the wonderfully fancy **Pritam Niwas Chowk** (Hall of the Beloved), known as Peacock Courtyard due to the dazzling colours of the patterned decorations around the four doorways'. It was built by the creator of the Hawa Mahal, Pratap Singh. Here, private music parties were held, observed by the royal harem from behind latticed screens upstairs. Each of the four doors represents a season and is embellished with scenes from Krishna's life. Beyond the courtyard lie the royal apartments that are closed to the public. Behind the palace, **Jai Niwas Bagh** gardens with the temple of **Govinda Deva** is popular with Hindu worshippers as well as peacocks and monkeys. Govinda is another name for Krishna when he is engaged in frolics with the *gopis*, his cowgirl-consorts. The temple was established by Jai Singh II who proclaimed Govinda the patron deity of Jaipur Rajputs. The City Palace is open daily from 09:30 to 16:45.

**Below** *Giant silver vessel at the City Palace.*

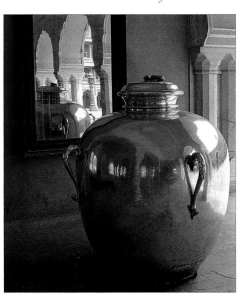

### JAALI

*Jaali* are latticework screens carved from slabs of stone and widely used in Indian architecture. They were first introduced by the Mughals who excelled at devising ways to cool down, including the celebrated *charbagh* or four-garden structure of waterways seen at the Taj Mahal and most Mughal tombs and palaces. The screens have a double function: they ensure privacy and enable fresh currents of air to circulate through them.

### Jantar Mantar ***

At first glance what looks like a futuristic sculpture park is in fact an ambitious and unique astronomical observatory. *Jantra* means instrument, *mantra* magic formula – but there is more science here than magic. The first open-air observatory in India was built earlier in Delhi by Jai Singh II, followed by other ones in Ujjain, Varanasi and Mathura. This Jantar Mantar is the largest and the only one made of stone. The gifted maharaja, Jai Singh II, was very much *au fait* with the latest trends in European science when construction began and was determined to build the most accurate instruments for measuring time in Hindustan. The 13 devices are complex and to get a grasp of the basic concepts you may want to hire a guide, available at the entrance, or refer to the brochure you will be given. Below is a summary of the main instruments.

**Nari Yantra** is a sundial consisting of two cylinders placed at an angle; the one to the north was used in winter, the other in summer. **Samrat Yantra** (supreme instrument) is the most imposing construction in the grounds, standing at 27m (90 feet). It is a giant sundial for measuring local time in hours, minutes and seconds.

It also measures meridian time, zenith distance and the altitude of celestial spheres. The local time was announced to the people of Jaipur with drums sounded at the top of the instrument's stairs. It is listed as the largest sundial in the *Guinness Book of Records*.

**Rashi Valaya Yantra** is a group of twelve instruments that correspond to the zodiac signs. They are more for fun than serious scientific purposes. **Jai Prakash Yantra** was Jai Singh's invention, which consists of two large concave marble spheres representing the celestial sphere upside-down. Their rims represent the horizon and are graduated at 360 degrees. Its function is to determine local time and the sun's path. **Ram Yantra** and **Digamsha Yantra** – huge circular devices – are compasses of a sort used to calculate azimuths (distances of celestial bodies) and altitudes. The **Yantra Raj** is an ancient metal astrolabe designed by Jai Singh. Its surface is inscribed with a diagram of the cosmos and it was used to calculate the height and position of celestial objects. It too, features in the *Guinness Book of Records* as the largest astrolabe in the world. Open 09:00–16:30 daily.

**Above:** *Nari Yantra, a sundial at Jantar Mantar.*
**Opposite:** *Jantar Mantar observatory conceived by the genius of Jai Singh II.*

### The Bazaars of Jaipur ★★★

The crafts of Jaipur constitute the city's economic back bone. The variety of products, density and size of the bazaars, uniqueness of some crafts and finesse of the artisans' work all make for an unmissable experience for the connoisseur as well as for the idle stroller. Jaipur is paradise for the compulsive shopper but also for the aesthete. Allow plenty of time to look for the best value and quality. If your time is very limited, make a trip to the **Rajasthan Government Handicrafts Emporium** on the Amber Road which is a reliable, fixed-price show-case of local crafts. Do not, however, trust the 'Government approved' sign outside various other shops along MI Road and Amber Road, although many have great stock.

The most obvious place to start is the tourist shopping area around Hawa Mahal, where you can buy anything from curios to gems – beware though, as this is definitely not the place to look for top quality or authenticity. **Johari Bazaar**, the oldest and liveliest market of the city, is a long succession of temples, grocers and gem dealers. Here, and along Gopalji Ka Bazaar off Johari Bazaar, is the lapidary centre of Jaipur – and indeed of India. You can watch cutters and polishers at their delicate craft, known as *meenakari*: the characteristic Jaipuri style of gem-inlaid gold. Do your homework before buying and go to a reputable dealer to make sure your diamonds are not zircon. Sapphires, rubies and emeralds are all very cheap and jewellery can be made to your own design. The established shop of **Bhuramal Rajmal Surana**, in a beautiful old *haveli* in Haldion ka Rasta (another lane off Johari Bazaar), is where some of the best designs and quality can be found. MI Road has a number of jewellers of which the most reliable is **Gem Palace** where the client's design can be made on the spot. Interesting silver jewellery can be found in Chameli Market opposite the Post Office in MI Road.

Jaipur and the nearby town of Sanganer are world-famous exporters of **textiles**. Tie-dye fabrics and **block-prints** are found in Johari Bazaar and you can see the dyers and printers at work in the district north of Ramganj Bazaar. **Arawali Textiles** off Amber Road is only one of many excellent textile shops where you can get clothes made for you from silk or cotton at a fraction

**Opposite:** Jootis *for sale in the streets of Jaipur.*
**Below:** *Puppets wait for customers in Deorhi Bazaar.*

of the European price. Take a garment or picture for the tailor to copy. There is a cluster of Rajasthani cloth shops in narrow lanes on the western side of Johari Bazaar, near Badi Chaupar. Good shops outside of the Pink City include **Anokhi** in Tilak Marg, southwest of MI Road, which has expensive Western-style clothes and **Maharaja Textile Printer** near Gangapol, the northern gate of the walled city. For more – and a closer look at the techniques – travel to **Sanganer**, 16km (10 miles) away (*see* page 86), also the home of handmade paper.

---

**BLUE POTTERY**

Blue pottery came to India with the first Mughal Babur. A Persian concept combined with Chinese glazing technique, blue tiles became part of Mughal architecture. The method was kept secret and an ever-diminishing number of craftsmen were privy to it, until it disappeared altogether. Only recently has it been revived by Kripal Singh, who travelled the world to rediscover this ancient technique and restore it to India. His studio is in west Jaipur and his apprentices work all over the area.

---

**Opposite:** *Sari seller in Jahari bazaar.*
**Below:** *Bangles for sale at a Jaipur bazaar.*

Leading to the east from the frantic and highly entertaining **Badi Chaupar**, the heart of the city where mass-produced items can be found, is **Ramganj Bazaar**, that specializes in traditional slip-on shoes and slippers known as *jootis*, These are mostly made of leather and sometimes embroidered. The best ones are made of camel hide. **Johari**, Bhawani Villa, Gulab Path, tel: (0141) 237 7037, is an excellent guaranteed leather outlet. North of Badi Chaupar is **Sire Deorhi Bazaar** where puppets are made and sold. If you haven't visited the **City Palace** yet, this is a good way: go through the **Sire Deorhi Gate** and into **Jaleb Chowk** square where you can have a refreshing drink at a café.

A unique craft flourishing here is the Jaipur blue pottery and tiles. The man who revived this ancient craft from the neglect of recent history is **Kripal Singh Shekhawat** whose studio is to the west of the Pink City, B-18a Shiva Marg, Bani Park, tel: (0141) 220 1127 – call for an appointment. You will need to take a taxi or autorickshaw there. His characteristic use of aquamarine blues and saturated colours, in addition to the classic blue and white tiles, is a pleasure for the eye. He also offers tourists lessons in pottery and miniature-painting. An offspring of blue pottery is **ceramic jewellery**, found in Neerja in Bhawani Singh Marg off Sawai Ram Singh Road in the south.

Other crafts well worth seeing are beautiful handmade paper, available at **Khadi Ghar** in MI Road; the intricate brassware enamelling at **PM Allah Buksh & Son** on MI Road; and sandalwood carving, miniature-painting and marble sculpture in **Khazne Wallon ka Rasta** off Chand Pol Bazaar.

Other popular bazaars are **Nehru Bazaar** and **Bapu Bazaar**, alongside the southern gates of the Pink City, selling bangles, local perfumes, block-printed cottons and shoes. **Tripolia Bazaar** west of Badi Chaupar and **Chaura Bazaar** which runs off it, sell textiles and more mundane objects. A note of caution: it is always safest to pay in cash, but if you have to pay by credit card, make sure you don't lose sight of your card. Scams have been known to occur here, especially in the gem trade.

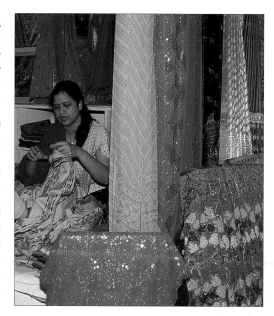

## Rajasthani Food

Rajasthani cuisine is characterized by two extremes: non-vegetarian at one end and strictly vegetarian at the other. Although eating out is a relatively recent phenomenon, the city's restaurants and hotels cater for both tastes. Entire communities, such as the Jains, are traditionally vegetarian. However, Rajput diet through the centuries has focused on meat. Mughlai cuisine, influenced by Mughal tastes and widely available in Jaipur, is also meat oriented. A typical Rajput meat dish consists of mutton, usually lamb or goat, roasted or minced, from which *keema* and *kebabs* are made. Probably the most appealing to visitors would be *sulla*, marinated lamb grilled on a skewer. Fish, white meat, pork, rabbit and partridge are also on the menus. Richness of flavours and an abundance of spices characterizes most Rajasthani meat dishes, although there are milder variations such as yoghurt-based seasoning. The staple food of the common people is *bajre ki roti* (millet bread),

### JEWELLERY

The women of Rajasthan are noted for their colourful clothes and heavy, elaborate jewellery. Some of the most brilliant silver jewellery is worn by the Banjaras or gypsy nomads. It is very fashionable in the cities – the heavy silver belts, bangles and anklets are copied by many fashion designers in Delhi and Bombay. Aside from the aesthetic value of adornment, there is an economic reason why women choose to wear kilograms worth of silver: it is a portable form of wealth. In the past, carrying one's wealth to protect it from looters was a very sensible thing indeed!

usually eaten with onions and chutney. A fancier meal might include *jhal* (potato curry) and fried white bread. Jaipur has a number of excellent vegetarian restaurants among them are **LMB**, **Chanakya**, **Four Seasons** – and some very good non-vegetarian ones like **Chowki Dhani** (22km [14 miles] out of town but worth the trip), **Niro's** and the **Copper Chimney**. The top hotels such as **Jai Mahal** and the **Rajputana Palace Sheraton** also have outstanding restaurants, some with outdoor dining and Indian music (*see* page 79).

## BEYOND THE PINK CITY

If you have an extra day, have a look at wider Jaipur. It provides welcome respite from the hectic pace of the city. Gardens, museums, cenotaphs, pavilions and temples all lie outside the walled city.

### Ram Niwas Gardens ***

Just outside New Gate, lie the gardens of Maharaja Ram Singh who, inspired by the worldliness of then capital Calcutta, undertook the construction of the site as a famine charity project in 1868. They house the magnificent **Albert Hall**, also known as Central Museum, and one of the first zoos in the country. The project was initially conceived to provide relief for the famine that followed one drought and it soon became the cultural hub of the city. On the way to Albert Hall you will pass the Gallery of Modern Art and a crocodile breeding farm which is part of the zoo, but in poor condition. Albert Hall, a fine colonial building, was inspired by the grandeur of the Victoria and Albert Museum in London and combines Indo-Saracenic motifs and Victorian styles.

---

**WHAT'S IN A COLOUR**

It used to be possible to define a person's status and origin by the colour and style of their turban or the jewels and pins decorating it. Thus, white was for *brahmins*, red for *kshatriyas*, brown for *vaishyas* and black for *shudras*. Today, Rajasthani turbans and saris are still distinguished by their bright colours and extravagant styles, but mainly give insight into the wearer's character and mood. Red – the warrior's colour – is still popular in Rajasthan. Blue succeeded white as the brahmins' colour, probably because it was the hue favoured by Krishna. Yellow (for mangoes) is the colour of spring and rejuvenation, pink in all its permutations is staple.

Today it houses the **Central Museum** (open 10:00–16:30 daily, except Friday), exhibiting local customs and crafts. In a separate room, the Durbar Hall displays rare carpets, including one of the most stunning ever made anywhere: a 17th-century Persian garden carpet whose colours are still vivid. Its design was based on the idea of the *charbagh* (*see* panel on page 103) or pleasure garden.

### Sisodia Rani ka Bagh

Passing through the southeast Ghat Gate and taking the road to Agra, you will reach **Vidyadharji ka Bagh** (about 8km [5 miles] from the city), a garden dedicated to the genius architect of Jaipur and the only remaining memorial to his life and achievement. Opposite it is the **Sisodia Rani ka Bagh**, a landscaped garden and country palace (one of the most beautiful in Rajasthan) built by Jai Singh II for one of his wives – a Rajput princess from the Sisodia clan whom he had married to strengthen political alliances. When relations between Jai Singh II and the Sisodia Rajputs deteriorated, the queen was

**Opposite:** *Charcoal-grilled sullas, a favourite Rajasthani speciality.*
**Below:** *The splendid Albert Hall.*

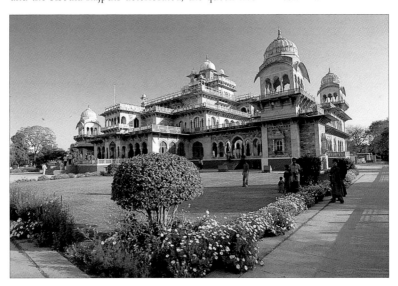

**Opposite:** *Rambagh
Palace, now one of India's
most sumptuous hotels.*
**Below:** *Sisodia Rani ka
Bagh, built by Jai Singh II
for his Rajput wife.*

exiled to a private residence outside the City Palace with
her son Madho Singh. The gardens are open 08:00–18:00,
the palace is usually closed and can only be seen from
the outside, but ask the guard to open up for you – it
still retains the lush atmosphere of a regal retreat.

## Galta Temples

The temples at **Galta** can be reached by the road leaving
from Suraj Pol to the east, or by driving on north from
Sisodia Rani ka Bagh. First on the way is the **Hanuman
Temple** – dedicated to the monkey god. The place is overrun with monkeys which are at their loudest and happiest
when the Hanuman priest arrives at 16:00 in a rickshaw
with sacks of bananas for their daily feast. Hanuman is one
of the most popular Hindu deities. Further up the road are
the water tanks – the upper used for bathing by people, the
lower by monkeys which have a protected status anywhere in proximity to a Hanuman temple. Although they
are friendly, avoid playing with them and giving them
food as they can carry rabies. The **Galta temples** are 250
years old and painted with entertaining religious scenes.
There are beautiful views over the surrounding plains.

## Gaitor Tombs

Some 4km (2 miles) off the main road to Amber and 6km (3 miles) from the City Palace are the marble *chhatris* (small, domed Mughal kiosks) or mausolea of Jaipur's rulers. The finest of them all is of course that of Jai Singh II, built by his son and successor Iswari Singh. It depicts Hindu mythological Hindu scenes and Jaipur landmarks including the Hawa Mahal. Iswari Singh himself was an ineffective ruler who took his life by swallowing poison and have a cobra bite him just to be sure. This suicide was prompted by the advance of the fierce Marathas – a tribe forever at war with the Rajputs. The maharaja's wives also responded: some took poison and the remaining 21 committed *sati* (self-immolation) on their husband's funeral pyre – which was a hasty affair, hence the absence of a tomb for this unfortunate ruler.

## Man Sagar Lake

This lake is a 10 minute drive travelling north from Gaitor Tombs, so it is best to stop by on your way to Amber or into Jaipur. One passes factory shops making and selling block-print, carpets, pottery and other fabrics. The, now inaccessible, romantic palace in the middle of the lake, Jal Mahal, was built by Jai Singh II's son Madho Singh I and used for duck shooting parties.

### RAMBAGH PALACE HOTEL

This palace began in the early 19th century as four pavilions that were turned into a hunting resort by Ram Singh and renamed Rambagh after him. Madho Singh's 11-year-old son Man Singh was kept and educated here, under British tutelage, away from the bad influences of the City Palace. Here, in 1931, the first male Rajput child in 100 years was born, an event that was celebrated with due pomp. Around that time, Man Singh met and fell in love with the 13-year-old daughter of a neighbouring Maharaja. She was Gayatri Devi – known as one of the most beautiful women of her time who became his wife eight years later. The palace was aggrandized for this occasion. The queen survived her husband who died in a polo accident and now lives in the Lily Pool Palace on the Rambagh grounds. Following Independence, in 1957, the palace was turned into the most sumptuous hotel of its kind in India, now run by the Taj Group of Hotels.

# Jaipur at a Glance

## BEST TIMES TO VISIT

Jaipur has a climate similar to that of Delhi. The heat, however, can be even more suffocating here in the pre-**monsoon** summer months of **May–June**, made even worse by devastating periodic **droughts** when the monsoon fails. The best time of the year to visit Jaipur is **October–March**. March is also the time of the fabulous **Elephant Festival**, a sight to behold.

## GETTING THERE

The **railway station** is about 1km west of the central city; rail information tel: 131, reservations 135. The **bus terminal** is closer, in Station Road; coach information, tel: (0141) 511 6031 and (0141) 510 8370. If **driving**, you'll probably arrive from the north, through Amber. There are also **flights** from Delhi, Mumbai, Kalkata and various Rajasthani cities, on Indian Airlines, tel: (0141) 274 3500/3324, and Jet Airways, tel: (0141) 511 2222-4. The airport is near Sanganer, 16km south of Jaipur.

## GETTING AROUND

Taxis and auto-rickshaws are the best transport. In smaller and cluttered areas, such as the bazaars within the walled city, cycle-rickshaws are a good option. You will need to bargain them down or use the pre-paid rank beside the bus station. It is worth hiring a good driver by the day or half day.

Heavy pollution and dusty wind blowing in from the Thar Desert in the summer can cause throat and lung problems so use enclosed taxis, preferably with air-conditioning. Within the Pink City, peak-hour traffic is horrendous and best avoided.

## WHERE TO STAY

Jaipur is best known for its regal accomodation – former palaces transformed into spectacular hotels that rate among the most original in the country. The less expensive *haveli* (town-house style) accommodation consists of refurbished noble mansions. While not always cheap, by Western standards, they are good value. There are also some budget options. Hotels are heavily booked around festival times, so it is best to prebook.

### LUXURY

**Hotel Welcome Rajputana Palace Sheraton**, Station Rd, Jaipur, tel: (0141) 240 1140; www.welcomgroup.com
A large super deluxe modern *haveli*-style hotel, with a pool, superb restaurants including the North-West Frontier Peshawri, a blow-out buffet at the Jal Mahal, and wonderful ice-creams in the coffee shop. Central. Also has an excellent bookshop, Bookwise (India) PVT Ltd, tel: (0141) 510 7255.
**Rambagh Palace** (*see* page 77), Bhawani Singh Marg, tel: (0141) 238 1919, www.tajhotels.com

Glorious palace-hotel, the former residence of the maharajas of Jaipur. Huge gardens, polo grounds, shops, restaurant. The suites are out of this world – and so are the prices. Cultural performances at night.
**Rajvilas**, Goner Road, Babaji ka More; tel: 0141-268 0101, www.rajvilas.com
Oberoi's luxurious Moghul fort, set in lush gardens; separate villas (with private pools) and tents as well as rooms. Elephant and horseback treks arranged.

### MID-RANGE

**Samode Haveli**, Gangapole, tel/fax: (0141) 263 2407, www.samode.com
Gorgeous, lushly decorative former residence of the Rawals of Samode. Impeccable service, restaurant; recommended.
**Shahpura House**, D257 Devi Marg, tel: 0141-220 2293, www.shahpurahouse.com
A fanciful wedding cake of a house. Rooftop restaurant, air conditioning and bathrooms in most rooms. Near station.
**Alsisar Haveli**, Sansar Chandra Road, tel: 0141-236 8290/4685, www.alsisar.com
Restored *haveli*, pool, terrace, good restaurant. Puppet and dance displays in the evening.

### BUDGET

**Arya Niwas**, Sansar Chandra Road, tel: (0141) 237 2456; www.aryaniwas.com
Efficiently run, all the basics. Good, reasonable vegetarian restaurant. Internet access.

# Jaipur at a Glance

**Bissau Palace**, Khetri House Rd, Chand Pol, tel: (0141) 230 4391; www.bissaupalace.com Atmospherically faded former residence of the Thakurs of Bissau, still run by their descendants; 28 rooms, gardens, badminton and tennis courts, pool and restaurant.
**Diggi Palace**, Diggi House, Shivaji Marg, tel: (141) 237 3091; email: diggihtl@datainfosys.net
Converted *haveli* in lovely garden near the SMS Hospital. Best are the detached cottages on the lawn. Good restaurant.

## WHERE TO EAT

Most of the best restaurants are in the hotels; try those in the Rajputana Palace Sheraton. Good hotels with excellent restaurants include the Jai Mahal Palace Hotel, Jacob Rd, which has veranda and lawn tables, and top *Mughlai* and North Indian cuisine; the Mansingh Hotel, off Sansar Chandra Marg, where there is outstanding Indian food, rooftop dining and *qawwali* singing (see panel page 52).
**Chowky Dhani**, south of Jaipur, take a taxi. Popular among wealthy locals, excellent Rajasthani food. Small entrance fee for the live entertainment. Open Mon–Sat 18:30–23:00, Sun to 14:30.
**Copper Chimney**, MI Road. *Mughlai* and North Indian cuisine, additional Western and Chinese menus. Try the rogan josh (medium spicy lamb curry).

**Dasaprakash**, 5 Kamal Mansions, MI Road (opp. Sagar Department Store). Branch of widespread chain. Vegetarian South Indian and continental food, plus an ice cream parlour.
**Four Seasons**, D-43A Subhash Marg, south of Prithvi Raj Rd, in residential district, very popular and cheap. Has great South and North Indian dishes, ice creams and shakes.
**Niro's**, MI Road, top-notch Indian food, plus vegetarian dishes and other options.
**Chanakya**, MI Road. Large, popular restaurant specializing in *thalis* and *parathas*. Open for lunch and dinner.
**LMB**, Johari Bazaar. Hugely successful, it prides itself on its pure Brahmin cooking: no garlic or onions. The ingredients are allegedly all ground and mixed on the premises, and everything is cooked in ghee (clarified butter). also has traditional desserts including mango and pistachio ice creams.
**Lassiwalla**, across from Niro's, MI Road. Popular in the summer, unmissable refreshment stop. *Lassi* is a delicious yoghurt drink, served sweet or salted.
**Mr Beans**, E-141A, C-Scheme, Sardar Patel Marg. The place to

hang out if you are desperate for a latte, popular with local yuppies. Coffee comes in 26 flavours – some taste of coffee!

## TOURS AND EXCURSIONS

Full- and half-day tours of Jaipur and environs are a good option. Book these, or your own government-approved guide, through your hotel, through the **Rajasthan Tourist Office** at the railway station (Platform 1) and at the Tourist Hotel, MI Road, tel: (0141) 511 0598 (open 08:00–20:00), or through the **Government of India Tourist Office**, Khasa Kothi Hotel, tel: (0141) 237 2200.
*Jaipur City Guide* and *Jaipur Vision* are both monthly listings guides with good up-to-date information, on sale at bookshops and newsagents.

## USEFUL CONTACTS

**Police**, tel: 100.
**SMS Hospital**, Sawai Ram Singh Road, tel: (0141) 256 4222.
**Thomas Cook** (for currency exchange), Jaipur Towers, M.I. Road, tel: (0141) 237 9422. There are also plenty of ATM machines.

| JAIPUR | J | F | M | A | M | J | J | A | S | O | N | D |
|---|---|---|---|---|---|---|---|---|---|---|---|---|
| AVERAGE TEMP. °C | 14 | 17 | 23 | 29 | 34 | 35 | 31 | 30 | 30 | 27 | 21 | 16 |
| AVERAGE TEMP. °F | 57 | 63 | 73 | 84 | 93 | 95 | 88 | 86 | 86 | 81 | 70 | 61 |
| HOURS SUN DAILY | 12 | 12 | 12 | 14 | 14 | 14 | 13 | 14 | 13 | 12 | 12 | 12 |
| RAINFALL mm | 14 | 8 | 9 | 4 | 10 | 54 | 193 | 239 | 90 | 19 | 3 | 4 |
| RAINFALL in | 0.5 | 0.3 | 0.4 | 0.2 | 0.4 | 2.1 | 7.5 | 9.3 | 3.5 | 0.7 | 0.1 | 0.2 |

# 4
# Around Jaipur

Jaipur is the capital of a state that abounds with interesting sights well worth the detour. As in the rest of India, distances in Rajasthan are too vast to enable quick access to some of the other fascinating towns, but the places listed below are all within half a day's road travel (at the most). Among these are some spectacular **natural reserves** rich in animal and birdlife, including tigers, crocodiles, cranes and eagles. There are craft villages and **palaces**. The highlight among these is the fort-palace of **Amber** (open 09:00–16:00 daily).

## AMBER FORT-PALACE

Overlooking a lake from an impregnable hill, the yellow **Amber Fort-Palace** is 11km (7 miles) north of Jaipur. One of the most majestic hilltop forts in Rajasthan, and perhaps all of India, it was the ultimate seat of Rajput power and a symbol of opulence. Begun by one aesthetic maharaja and finished by another, its peak of glory in the 16th and 17th centuries coincided with the flourishing of the Rajput-Mughal alliance.

The **Kachhawaha Rajputs** who claimed descent from one of the sons of god Rama, took over Amber after defeating the previous tribal rulers, the **Susawat Minas**, in the mid-12th century. It was not until the 16th century, however, that Amber fort came into existence. The enlightened Mughal emperor Akbar forged friendly relations with the proud Rajputs by marrying the daughter of the then ruler of Amber thus marking the beginning of centuries of prosperity in Rajputana.

---

### DON'T MISS

**\*\*\* Amber Fort-Palace:** situated on a hill it offers panoramic views of Maota Lake and the old town below.
**\*\*\* National parks:** enjoy a tiger safari and admire the scenery at **Ranthambhore** and **Sariska**.
**\*\* Jaigarh** and **Nahargarh forts:** great views.
**\*\* Samode Palace:** stay in this luxurious hotel.
**\*\* Alwar:** visit the palace.
**\* Sanganer:** noted for its fine block-printed textiles and paper.

---

**Opposite:** *The south end of Amber Fort-Palace with Jaigarh Fort on the hill.*

Amber rulers were given positions of power in the Mughal court and army. With the incredible wealth accumulated as a result, Maharaja Man Singh built the first palace of Amber, now at the back end of the complex, and a shrine to the goddess Kali that is still in use today. A great patron of the arts, Man Singh established a thriving community of craftsmen who specialized in ceramics, block-printing, enamelling and paper-making – a tradition that lives on in Amber and Jaipur.

Half a century later Jai Singh I, who ascended to the throne of Amber at the age of 12, expanded the palace into what forms the glorious front section of the complex today. The Mughlai architectural and cultural influence can be seen clearly in many aspects of the palace, such as the mirror inlay, the double-bracket supports on pavilion-like buildings, and the cooling water system inside, making it a visual celebration of a mighty political and cultural alliance. The shift of the Rajput seat of power from Agra to Jaipur in the 18th century is similar to that of the Mughal throne moving from Agra to Delhi in the 17th.

From the small tourist complex on the main Amber road, access to the fort towering above is by foot, elephant or car. Of these, the most dignified – if it isn't too hot – is the pleasant fifteen-minute hike up the winding stairs occupied by buskers, beggars and pigs. If you want to sit on an elephant, you can do so in the main courtyard of the fort, **Jaleb Chowk**, which is entered through the **Suraj Pol** (Sun Gate) that is a reminder of the divine provenance of the Kachhawahas. Before passing through **Singh Pol** (Lion Gate) at the top of the stairs and into the palace

## KALI, GODDESS OF WAR

Kali, the Hindu goddess of war and destruction, is an aspect of Durga, herself an aspect of Parvati, Shiva's consort. Kali is most often portrayed with 10 arms, skulls hanging around her neck and blood dripping from her mouth. Sometimes she dances on the body of Shiva or of vanquished demons. Animal sacrifices to Kali were common practice in Rajputana, performed in order to pacify her wrath. The last maharaja of Jaipur, Man Singh II, would occasionally drive in his jeep to Kali Mata Mandir at Amber to sacrifice a live goat.

complex, take a peek at **Kali Mata Mandir** to the right, a temple to Sila Mata, yet another incarnation of the bloodthirsty goddess, Kali, who was popular with the Rajputs. It was built by Man Singh I in 1604 and is still in use. The second courtyard's main feature is the stunning, red sandstone Mughal-style **Diwan-i-Am** (Hall of Public Audience), the most ambitious addition by Jai Singh. The third and largest gate, **Ganesh Pol**, which leads into the private apartments, is a magnificent building in itself and a triumph of the Rajasthani and Mughal decorative blend: painted floral motifs, images of gods, glass mosaics (possibly modelled on the Mughal tilework) and *jaali* (carved screens) above the gate, through which the royal ladies observed the comings and goings of the court. A diminutive, plump Ganesh, the elephant god of prosperity and happiness, is painted above the entrance. The courtyard has a landscaped, Mughal-style *charbagh* garden. To the right is **Sukh Niwas** (House of Pleasure), equipped with a system of fountains, where the royals retired on hot days. It was said to have the

> **THE HALL OF PUBLIC AUDIENCE**
>
> The Diwan-i-Am at the Amber palace is unmistakably Mughal in style, reminiscent of those in Agra, Delhi and Fatehpur Sikri. The concept of having separate buildings for different activities is also Mughal, and is again seen in the City Palace in Jaipur.

**Below:** *Amber Fort-Palace, Ganesh Pol, a triumph of decorative art.*

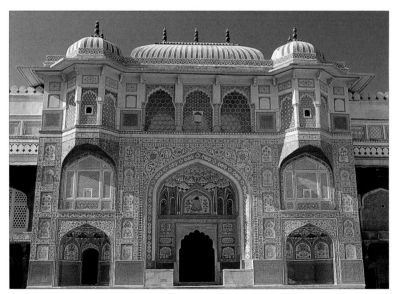

**Below:** *The exquisite interior of Nahargarh Fort.*

most beautiful among Rajput decorations. To the left is **Jai Mahal** (Hall of Victory), the royal private rooms. At ground level is the most splendid room of the palace – the **Sheesh Mahal** (Mirror Hall). Its marble walls and ceiling are inlaid with small pieces of mirror and coloured glass among bursts of floral engravings, creating the dazzling impression of a room full of jewels. Upstairs is Jai Singh's private apartment, **Jas Mandir** (Temple of Glory). Intricately decorated with mosaics and with a view to Lake Maota below, it has exquisite alabaster *jaali* at floor level. A climb up to the second storey of Ganesh Pol reveals a view to the courtyard below through the latticed screens where the royal harem once sat and observed.

The palace of Man Singh I lies through a small doorway at the far end of the gardens. He built 12 apartments or *zenana* (women's quarters) one for each of his wives, situated all around this fourth and last courtyard. Some remaining blue tile-work and paintings on the walls give an indication of the extent of the decorative work carried out under his orders.

## NAHARGARH FORT

Also known as Tiger Fort, **Nahargarh** (floodlit at night) is close to the royal *chhatris* at Galta, along a ridgeroad off Amber Road that offers great views of the romantic duck-hunting pavilion, Jal Mahal, in Man Sagar Lake. The fort was built by Jai Singh II in 1734 as a defence post for the brand-new city of Jaipur. Here, where local time was announced with gunshots, the royal ladies came to cool off during summer (in

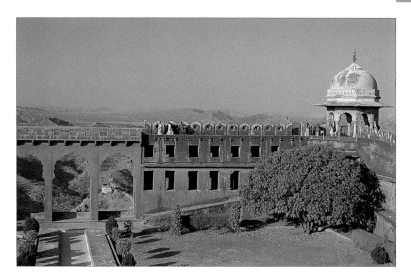

the mid-19th century Ram Singh built more apartments for his wives). The spectacular views over Jaipur and the fine decorations in the halls are well worth the effort. Open from 10:00–22:00 daily. There is also a small restaurant and a rest room at the top of the fort.

**Above:** *Jaigarh Fort offers breathtaking views.*

## JAIGARH FORT

South of Amber Fort is the older fort of **Jaigarh**, home of the Kachhawaha rulers before Amber was built. The Kachhawaha treasure was kept here – ironically the treasurers were the defeated Meenas, previous lords of Amber. Only the maharaja's family had access to the fort. Here is found the largest cannon in India, **Jai Van** (Voice of Victory), whose barrel is decorated with elephants, birds and flowers. Built by Jai Singh II, it needed 100kg (221 pounds) of gun powder for each shot and when tested, the ball was found 38km (24 miles) away; this was the first and last time it was ever used. For those interested in weapons, the foundry – unique in India – is fully equipped with moulds, a kiln and more cannons on display. The palace has several halls and spectacular views. Open 09:00–16:30 daily.

### THE KACHHAWAHA TREASURE

The unimaginable treasure of the Kachhawaha Rajputs was kept in their former residence Jaigarh Fort, where it was loyally guarded by their defeated enemies, the Meenas. Out of this wealth were born the palaces of Amber and Jaipur. Each newly appointed ruler was brought to the treasury blindfolded and allowed to take just one object for himself. Madho Singh II picked up a bird made from solid gold, with rubies for eyes and a large emerald in its beak. Attempts to excavate the buried treasure have been fruitless.

**Right:** *Block-printing is done using wooden blocks dipped in dye and printed onto cloth.*

## SANGANER

This town 16km (10 miles) south of Jaipur is a hub of **textile production**, block-printing in particular being its trademark. Here you can watch the practice of an age-old tradition of handmade fabrics and designs – and purchase them at lower prices. Fabric is soaked in vats of hot dye, stirred, drained, then rinsed, sometimes soaked in cow dung to aid bleaching, and finally spread out in the sun for three days. Block-printing is a simple technique consisting of repetitively applying different-shaped wooden blocks to the fabric after dipping them in dye. The skill is in the precision of the application and the equal colouring of each print. While some producers prefer to use cheaper commercial chemicals, others, such as the famous label Anokhi, stick to natural vegetable dyes. Most textile shops are found along the main road. In addition, there are workshops making beautiful paper from the cotton and silk left-overs of the textile industry and hand-printed pottery in blue, white and green. There are a number of Jain and Krishna temples in the town.

## RANTHAMBHORE NATIONAL PARK

Nowhere in India are you more likely to spot a tiger than in the Ranthambhore National Park, some 161km (100 miles) south of Jaipur. Due to the constant proximity of jeeps filled with tiger-watchers, these most majestic of animals are not shy; sometimes they will hunt, drink

---

### PROJECT TIGER

At the turn of the 20th century there were around 40,000 tigers in India. Tragically, this number has been reduced to about 4000, up from a low of about 1500. Tiger hunting has always been a sport for the wealthy and Mughals and Rajputs alike indulged in this favourite of pastimes. It was the British, however, who surpassed all in their unrelenting pursuit of trophies, often posing with tiger corpses for photographs. Poaching too has had a devastating effect. With the introduction of **Project Tiger** in the 1970s, measures were taken to improve management and care. Half of the existing tigers live outside of the reserves that were created to protect them.

from one of the marshy lakes, or simply lounge about while crowds of avid tourists snap pictures of them. At present it is estimated that there are about 45 tigers at Ranthambhore, but as the reserve is quite large, seeing one is not guaranteed and you may have to try more than once. At least one overnight stay is recommended. January to April is the best time to try, as this is the dry season when tigers come out to the lakes. The park has a wealth of other animals – leopard (more difficult to spot), jackal, chital, crested serpent eagle, deer, sloth bear, wild boar and crocodile. The latter can be spotted in the marshes on the side of the road, where ruined, moss-covered temples rise out of stagnant waters as if out of a dream. The park was once used as hunting grounds by Rajput rulers seated on elephants.

## SAMODE PALACE

Approximately 42km (26 miles) north of Jaipur, west of the main road to Delhi, stands the yellow, decadent 18th century palace-hotel of Samode. It rose to fame in the late 1980s when a romantic film, *The Far Pavilions,* was shot here. It is situated in the midst of bare hills topped with forts and is ideal for a night's retreat, complete with candlelight rooftop dinner. The lords of Samode, loyal to the rulers of Jaipur, traced their origins to a prince of the Kachhawaha Rajputs and the youngest heirs still own the palace. The glittering **Sheesh Mahal** is reminiscent of its

> **BROTHERLY INTRIGUE**
>
> Sanganer was where Jai Singh II and his power-hungry half-brother Vijay Singh met, in the presence of their mother, to reach an agreement over Vijay's claims to the throne of Amber. The queen mother's courtiers, however, turned out to be disguised soldiers. No sooner had Jai Singh promised to fulfil his brother's demands, than Vijay found himself locked away in a room. Jai Singh II proceeded to create the city of Jaipur, becoming the most distinguished scholar, scientist, humanist and aesthete of all Rajput rulers.

**Below:** *A tiger lying at Ranthambhore National Park and Tiger Reserve.*

**THE ELEPHANT GOD**

Ganesh, the good-natured, elephant-headed son of Shiva and Parvati, is a symbol of knowledge, good fortune and success. The most popular deity among Hindus, his image is ubiquitous throughout India. Jaipur's Elephant Festival is a spectacular event, during which the bejewelled beasts parade through the city to the sound of drums. The elephants which transport tourists at Amber belong to special elephant unions.

namesake at Amber palace. The village of Samode produces tie-and-dye and block-printed fabrics, miniature painting and lacquered bangles.

## SARISKA NATIONAL PARK

Surrounded by Sariska wildlife sanctuary and similar to Ranthambhore, this park is home to a current estimate of about 25 tigers, as well as chital, wild boar, mongoose, and a variety of birds. There is a temple to Hanuman and the atmospheric ruins were once buildings used by the maharaja hunters. It is an alternative to the more famous Ranthambhore Reserve, depending on which way you are travelling.

## ALWAR

If you stop to see Sariska, Alwar is only 37km (23 miles) north on the way to Delhi and worth taking a couple of hours to explore. The **City Palace**, set on huge lush grounds, holds a **museum** and has a view of the large tank surrounded by elegant *ghats* and three-storeyed pavilions. There is also a fine marble-and-sandstone cenotaph **Moosi Maharani ki Chhatri**, that was built to commemorate the *sati* (self-immolation by fire) carried out on a local ruler's funeral pyre by his mistress. At night, the gates of the palace used to be closed to protect the town from tigers.

**Below:** *Elephant polo was a sport that was favoured by maharajas.*

# Around Jaipur at a Glance

## BEST TIMES TO VISIT

The heat can be suffocating in the pre-monsoon summer months, **May–Jun**, made even worse by devastating periodic **droughts** when the monsoon fails. The best time of the year to visit Jaipur is **Oct–Mar**. March is also the time of the fabulous **Elephant Festival**, a sight to behold.

## GETTING THERE

Amber, Jaigarh and Nawalgarh are easily reached by **car**. **Buses** to these forts, as well as to all the other destinations in this chapter, leave Jaipur every day; buses to Amber leave from the Hawa Mahal every 30 mins. If comfort is a priority, use a privately run luxury bus; tel: (0141) 511 6031 or 510 8370. Alwar, Sanganer, Sariska and Ranthambhore are well connected with Jaipur and each other by bus and **railway** networks. Make railway bookings at least a day in advance at the main station near Station Road; rail information tel: 131, reservations 135. When visiting Samode, travel by car or bus.

## GETTING AROUND

Ranthambhore and Sariska game-viewing tours are only possible in a pre-booked jeep or truck, run by the National Parks; door-to-door pickup service. Otherwise, for Alwar and Sanganer, taxis or rickshaws are useful if walking proves too much. If travelling by train, take a taxi to your hotel.

## WHERE TO STAY AND EAT

Overnight stops are recommended in Ranthambhore, Samode and Sariska.

### LUXURY

**Sawai Madhopur Lodge**, Ranthambhore Road, Sawai Madhopur, tel: (07462) 220 541; wwwtajhotels.com Former hunting lodge of Man Singh II, now a luxurious hotel with splendid gardens, restaurant, bar and swimming pool. Also offers expensive tents.

**Vanyavilas**, Ranthambhore Road, Sawai Madhopur, tel: (07462) 224 999; www.oberoihotels.com Luxurious air-conditioned tented rooms with private gardens and sundecks surround a building designed as a sumptuous royal hunting lodge, all set amongst lush gardens, with a pool, spa and lake.

**Samode Palace-Hotel**, Samode, tel: (0141) 263 2370, www.samode.com Regularly listed amongst the world's finest heritage hotels. An incredible setting, candle-lit verandah dinners, sumptuous Raj murals and furniture (see page 87). Pool, spa, and cultural performances.

**Sariska Palace**, Sariska District, tel: (0144) 284 1322, www.sariska.com Former maharaja's palace, modestly dubbed 'lodge' by him. Opposite park entrance. Has a pool, gym, yoga centre, lovely garden, beautiful furnishings and verandahs.

### MID-RANGE/BUDGET

**Ankur Resort**, Ranthambhore Road, tel: (07462) 220 792, fax: (07462) 223 303. Set in a garden, good value for clean rooms and reasonable food.

**Hotel Tiger Safari Resort**, Ranthambore Road, tel: (07462) 221 137. Pleasant little hotel with a rooftop restaurant, rooms with wall paintings and some separate cottages.

## TOURS AND EXCURSIONS

Amber, Jaigarh Fort and Nawalgarh Fort are included as part of the usual Jaipur tours. Ranthambhore National Park can only be entered by jeep or truck which must be booked the day before either from your hotel or, if you travel by train to the town of Sawai Madhopur which is on the way to Ranthambhore, at the Project Tiger office near the railway station. The safari runs twice daily, at 06:30 and 15:30 in summer, 07:00 and 14:30 in winter. Sariska can be entered by jeep, at 07:00 and 15:00 daily. Book at your hotel or one of the many travel agents in Jaipur.

## USEFUL CONTACTS

**Ranthambore Tourist Information**, RTDC Vinayak Tourist Complex, Ranthambore Road; tel: (07462) 220 808. Open Mon–Sat 10:00–13:00, 13:30–17:00.

**Project Tiger**, Ranthambore Road, Sawai Madhopur; tel: (07462) 223 402.

# 5
# Agra

Today, the earliest Mughal garden, the Ram Bagh, is dry but you can still see the symmetrical design and the fruit trees, cypresses and poplars that Babur, and later his great-grandson Jahangir, planted. There are pavilions and perfect geometrical pools and terraces.

## THE MUGHALS

The Mughals hailed from central Asia and had Turkish and Mongol blood in their veins. Babur, the founder of the empire of the Mughals in north India, was the ruler of the tiny central Asian kingdom of **Ferghanain**. He was a military adventurer who looked towards India for its wealth. In **1526** he defeated **Ibrahim Lodi**, the last of the Lodi sultans to rule north India at the famous **Battle of Panipat**. He then established Mughal control from **Kabul** to **Delhi** and **Agra**. Babur made Agra his capital, but his son **Humayun** moved to Delhi for a few years where he built his own city called **Dinpanah**. **Akbar**, Humayun's son, returned to Agra. The city was at its most powerful in the 16th and 17th centuries. In 1648, Akbar's grandson **Shah Jahan** relocated to Delhi where he built **Shahjahanabad**, and from this time Agra began to decline. It was finally conquered by the **Jats** (a prosperous rural community who live in north India) in 1761 and by the British in 1803.

After Babur died, his son Humayun inherited the Mughal throne. Humayun was also a valiant soldier but Mughal power had still not been consolidated and he spent most of his short reign in battle with the rulers of

---

**DON'T MISS**

**\*\*\* Agra Fort:** the seat of Mughal power during the 16th and 17th centuries.
**\*\*\* The Taj Mahal:** included in the list of the world's seven wonders. A must-see, especially at dusk or dawn.
**\*\*\* Old City:** stroll through the Old City in Agra and see artisans busy at work.
**\*\* Itimad-ud-Daulah's Tomb:** visit this lovely tomb situated on the east bank of the Jamuna River.

---

**Opposite:** *The Taj Mahal, one of the world's greatest architectural wonders.*

## PIETRA DURA

*Pietra dura*, a technique borrowed from Florence, is the name given to the **floral patterns** that the Mughals used to decorate their luxuriant architecture. They were lovers of nature, particularly gardens and flowers. *Pietra dura* became a special feature of Indo-Islamic architecture; the characteristic flowers and fruit motifs are not normally associated with Islamic buildings. *Pietra dura* is created from coloured stones such as marble, yellow, red and grey sandstone, lapis lazuli, as well as black slate. Tulips, lilies, irises and poppies were delicately inlaid in spray and arabesque patterns on a white marble background. This produced a richly ornamental look best exemplified in the Taj Mahal. Under torchlight, the stones glow with deep colour. *Pietra dura* work continues to be created by the descendants of the Taj Mahal craftsmen, and is nowadays also used to decorate contemporary items.

Gujarat and with Afghan chieftains like **Sher Shah**. Humayun was deposed by Sher Shah in 1540, but won Delhi and Agra back in 1555.

It was Babur's grandson Akbar who took the Mughal empire to its greatest heights. '*The eyes are small but extremely vivid ... reveal a sharpness of mind and a keenness of intellect,*' wrote **Father Monserrate**, a visiting Jesuit missionary, about Akbar in 1580. Akbar conquered Rajputana in the west and parts of Bengal in the east, the Deccan in the south and Kashmir in the north. He created enormous prestige for the Mughal crown and developed efficient administrative systems like the *mansabdari* practice by which potentially rebellious Rajput and Afghan nobles were co-opted into the Mughal government. He realized the importance of integration and although a Muslim, married a Rajput princess, **Jodhai Bai** with whom he had his first son, **Jahangir**. He created a new religion – the *Din-i-Ilahi*, or *Sulh-i-Kul* (Peace to All) – in which all sectarian divisions were to be disregarded in supreme duty to a single god and emperor.

Akbar's son, **Jahangir**, who became emperor in 1605, was an equally able ruler, although addicted to drink and opium. His celebrated romance with a beautiful courtesan named **Anarkali**, is the stuff of legends and famous Bollywood films. During Jahangir's reign, the Mughal state became a lavish patron of the arts. Portraiture, music and architecture flourished under Jahangir. The great artist **Mansur** painted the famous Mughal miniature birds at this time. Jahangir's most beautiful and powerful wife **Nur Jahan** built Agra's **Itimad-ud-Daulah** tomb, an extravagantly decorated structure, for her father. At this time,

Sir Thomas Roe, envoy of James I, received a royal letter from Jahangir allowing trade between the **East India Company** and India.

Jahangir was succeeded by his son **Shah Jahan**, the great builder who ensured the architectural glory of Mughals. Shah Jahan built the Red Fort in Delhi and, of course, the Taj Mahal – a mausoleum for his beloved wife **Mumtaz Mahal**. By the time Shah Jahan's son **Aurangzeb** came to the throne, the Mughal empire was over-extended and beginning to crumble under its own weight. Aurangzeb, the last great Mughal, was a controversial emperor. After Aurangzeb, the rulers who succeeded Aurangzeb were unable to maintain the

**Opposite:** *Agra Fort, the Mughals' seat of power in the 16th and 17th centuries.*

empire in the face of threats from the Marathas, and later the British. They were further weakened by infighting and decadent living. The last Mughal, **Bahadur Shah Zafar** was deposed and exiled to **Burma** by the British where he died in 1862.

**Above:** *Exterior of Amar Singh Gate.*

## AGRA FORT

The first building at this site was called **Badalgarh** and was probably built by a Rajput ruler called Badal Singh. Later the Lodis built a fort here, which had fallen to ruin by the time Akbar commissioned his fort. Situated on the banks of the Yamuna River, this massive red sandstone structure was the seat of Mughal power during the reigns of three of the greatest Mughals – Akbar, his son Jahangir and grandson Shah Jahan. It was built by Akbar, extended by Jahangir and completed by Shah Jahan. The complete range of Mughal architectural styles can be seen in the fort, from military toughness to artistic embellishment. There are heavy sandstone walls, battlements and great gates, as well as delicate marble pavilions, marble basins, decorated walls and the characteristic *jaali* work.

Under Akbar's rule the fort was primarily a military stronghold with formidable walls and battlements. Jahangir gave it its perfumed fountains and ornamental baths. Shah Jahan added his imprimatur by adding white marble pillars and arches. Besides being the royal residence, Agra fort throbbed with military power. The grand ramparts enclosed an army well supplied with food and artillery. A moat runs along the outer and inner walls and the huge towers were designed for attacking approaching enemies. Agra Fort is a poignant building. It was here that emperor Aurangzeb imprisoned his father Shah Jahan, leaving the old man to gaze upon his beloved Taj Mahal from the Jasmine Tower as he slowly died.

The main entrance to the Fort, reached across the drawbridge, is through the huge **Amar Singh Gate**. In the first quadrangle, you will see the huge stone bath directly in front of Akbar's palaces. This bath was probably used by Jahangir's wife Nur Jahan, who, it is said, bathed in water scented with rose petals and is credited with inventing the sickly sweet Mughal perfume known as *attar*. The **Jahangir Mahal** which Akbar built for his first wife Jodhai Bai, mother of Jahangir and princess of the Rajput state of Amber, shows a combination of Islamic and Hindu styles. The palace is richly carved with floral patterns, birds and intricate patterns. Blue-and-gold stucco paintings also decorate the walls. On the riverfront, there is a long open pavilion, in fact, the main verandah of the Jahangir Mahal, where the breezes coming from the river have a cooling effect and provide a beautiful view of the opposite bank. Akbar is said to have lived in the Jahangir Mahal when he was not away on military campaigns. There are rooms for his harem, his library and his own living quarters.

Other, equally richly decorated palaces lie near the Jahangir Mahal: **Khas Mahal** (Unique Palace) and **Sheesh Mahal** (Mirror Palace), built as imperial lodgings. These are spacious and richly decorated with niches for lamps and with enclosed doorways. Khas Mahal was known as Shah Jahan's *aram garh* or relaxation room. Outside the Khas Mahal is the **Anguri Bagh** or grape garden that is surrounded with rooms for court women. The Mughals were from central Asia and unused to the heat of the Indian plains. Deep darkened rooms, interspersed with fountains, were designed for coolness and to provide maximum protection from the sun's glare.

The **Musamman Burj** or **Jasmine Tower** has been described as a palace 'hanging like a fairy bower over the grim ramparts'. Its central room has a marble basin and a giant fountain, its walls are covered in *pietra dura* and *jaalis* and set with niches for lamps and vases. It was a grim irony that

### AMAR SINGH'S LEAP

The main gate of Agra Fort is Amar Singh Gate, named after a Rajput nobleman at the court of emperor Shah Jahan. Amar Singh committed an unpardonable error by slaying the royal treasurer for having slighted him in front of the emperor. Distraught at his own recklessness he rode his horse over the fort walls. The horse died and the hot-blooded Rajput was executed, but Shah Jahan was so impressed by this dramatic act that he named the main gate of the palace after him.

**Below:** *Red stone carving being restored.*

Taj Mahal

this fabulous palace, built by Shah Jahan, would one day become his prison, where he would live out the last of his days tended by his devoted daughter Jahanara.

The **Diwan-i-Am** (Hall of the People) and **Diwan-i-Khas** (Hall of the Noblemen) are built on a grand scale, again decorated with columns and carved walls. The emperor heard grievances of the people in the colonnaded Diwan-i-Am, seated on his famous **Peacock Throne**, which is said to have been set with rubies, diamonds and other precious stones. The Diwan-i-Khas – overlooking a long riverside verandah and situated on the terrace above the Mussaman Burj a floor above the Diwan-i-Am – was reserved for important guests. There are two thrones at the Diwan-i-Khas, one white and one black. The latter was created specially for Jahangir when he became emperor after a long wait and several rebellions against his father, at the age of 35.

Don't miss the **Machchi Bhavan** or Fish House, a large sunken fish pond with surrounding harem quarters. Meena Bazaar, situated at the northern side of the fort, was a market offering handicrafts and precious stones, and a lively evening spot for the inhabitants of the mosque, where the emperors flirted with courtesans. It was here that Jahangir met his **Nur Jahan** and Shah Jahan his **Mumtaz Mahal**.

The **Moti Masjid** (Pearl Mosque), built by Shah Jahan, is a blindingly white marble mosque located deep within the rooms of the Fort. It was a private place of worship for the nobility. Open daily, sunrise to sunset.

## THE TAJ MAHAL

For first time visitors and the local traveller, it's impossible not to be struck by the ethereal sad beauty of the Taj Mahal. The most cynical of world travellers have been silenced by this stunning structure that is almost vulnerable in its purity. The elegant white marble, slim minarets and floating dome create a sense of untouched romance, 'the proud passion of an emperor's love', as **Edwin Arnold** enthused. Of course, Shah Jahan would have been horrified at the pollution levels of modern Agra, a city now classified by the World Health Organization as 'pollution intensive zone'. With sections of the Taj's white marble becoming discoloured and brittle, experts have been giving it an ayurvedic face pack of fuller's earth, cereal, milk and lime, with spectacular results. Over 200 industries have been ordered to move out of this area, and cars, buses and scooters are banned within a 500m (1641 feet) radius of the Taj, but Agra remains a highly congested and polluted city and the fumes may one day take their toll on this most beautiful of India's buildings. For the moment, however, it certainly appears as dazzling as it has always been, well worth more than one single visit.

The love story of the emperor Shah Jahan and Noor Mahal, or Mumtaz Mahal, is well known throughout India. Shah Jahan, or Prince Khurram, as he was known before he ascended the throne, fell madly in love with the beautiful Arjumand Banu Begum, married her and gave her the title Mumtaz Mahal (Exalted one of the Palace). When she died in 1631 while giving birth to her 14th child, the emperor was so distraught that he mourned her death for two years, his hair turned grey overnight and he even stopped eating meat or listening to music. Quite a sacrifice for the high living Mughals! He promised to build the most beautiful mausoleum ever known to the world. After it was commissioned, the Taj took 22 years to build. It cost nearly 400 million rupees, used 500kg (1103 pounds) of gold, and approximately 20,000 men and women toiled

### UNHAPPY FAMILIES

Architecture and military glory aside, the Mughals have gone down in history as a succession of big, unhappy families. But no Mughal could compete with the grim, fanatical Aurangzeb who managed to eliminate all the males in his family in an effort to obtain and keep his throne. First, he incarcerated his younger brother Murad who was an opium addict. His elder brother, and favourite of Shah Jahan and the people, Darah Sukoh, was mercilessly pursued, put to death, and his head presented to their heartbroken father. Aurangzeb also ordered the imprisonment and execution of Darah Sukoh's handsome son at Gwalior Fort. He finally removed his own father from the throne and imprisoned him at Agra Fort, where the great Shah Jahan spent his last years gazing disconsolately at the distant Taj Mahal that contained the remains of his beloved Mumtaz. Critics blame Aurangzeb for his religious intolerance which, after centuries of harmony, spelt the beginning of the end for the Mughal empire.

**Left:** *Entrance gateway to the Taj Mahal.*

on it. All the marble was imported from Rajasthan, turquoise from Persia and diamonds from central Asia. The names of the architects are unknown. Some sources say that the chief architect was one **Ustad Ahmad Lahori**, others say it was Persian **Isa Khan**. Designers were brought in from overseas – Mohammad Afandi from Turkey, Mullah Mushid from Persia and Geronimo Veroneo, whose grave can be found in the Roman Catholic cemetery in Agra, from Venice.

The original entrance to the Taj was a huge red sandstone arch which housed a market complex. You cannot enter through this gate anymore, but by a small door to the right where you are frisked by security guards. The gateway is inscribed with verses from the 89th chapter of the Qur'an, one of which reads: '*So enter as one of his servants, and enter into his garden.*'

The Taj was built to resemble paradise on earth and the doors of the gateway were apparently once made of solid silver that was later plundered by invading tribes of **Jats**. As you enter, you see the first picture postcard view of the Taj, floating above the ground, its great dome deceptively near. The garden, divided into eight squares in the *charbagh* style is laid out along the central waterway in front of the mausoleum. Rows of cypresses line this long canal and the lotus pool, named after the lotus-shaped fountain spouts. The perfectly symmetrical reflection of the Taj in the water of the lotus pool emphasizes the marvel of its architecture.

The Taj stands on a marble platform about 8m (22 feet) high and covering an area of 95m² (313 square feet). Since you cannot see the platform from the gateway, it looks as if the mausoleum is floating. Up close, the staggering detail of the carvings, *pietra dura* lilies and tulips, Qur'anic inscriptions, inlaid precious and semi-precious

**Above:** *The Taj Mahal with local children in the foreground near the Mehtab Bagh.*
**Opposite:** *Replicas of the cenotaphs of Mumtaz Mahal and Shah Jahan.*

stones – most of them vandalized and gouged out by now – show the care and attention that the artisans lavished on this building. Four small domes surround the central dome of the Taj. Directly below the central dome in the octagonal burial chamber lie the false cenotaphs of Mumtaz Mahal and Shah Jahan. The real ones are housed in a basement directly beneath. The burial chamber is lit by daylight filtering through marble *jaalis* and is superbly decorated with *pietra dura* and **Qur'anic** inscriptions. It has been said that the only discordant note in the Taj is, ironically enough, the tomb of Shah Jahan which his son Aurangzeb placed next to that of Mumtaz. The building was designed so that Mumtaz's tomb would be its single centrepiece under the central dome – Shah Jahan's tomb breaks the pattern.

On either side of the Taj stand two sandstone edifices – a mosque and what was probably a royal guesthouse. The mosque is impressive, but pales in comparison to the Taj.

Some say that Shah Jahan planned a black Taj on the opposite bank of the Yamuna, but there is no evidence that construction was ever begun on such a structure.

Sunrise and sunset are the best times to visit the Taj Mahal. The marble catches and reflects the light in such a manner that it would seem as though the architects and designers were seeking some sort of union with the sun and moon, so that their creation would complement the movements of the heavenly bodies. The Taj has been described the Islamic concept of paradise.

Across the river from the Taj, a Mughal garden, the **Mehtab Bagh**, is being restored. It's a wonderful place from which to watch the sunset, with superb views of the Taj.

---

**ENTRY TO THE TAJ**

The Taj is open 06:00–19:00 every day except Monday. At the time of writing, the ticket is Rs750 for foreigners, but this gives a discount at all other Agra monuments visited on the same day. For five days a month, surrounding the full moon, the Taj opens from 20:30 to 00:30. Tickets are only available in advance from the Archaeology Survey of India (see page 105). The Taj museum is open every day except Monday and Friday and entry is free. It contains lithographs of the Taj, old photographs and information on the materials used in the construction.

**Above:** *A craftsman fashions a table using the pietra dura technique.*
**Opposite:** *Inside, Agra Fort is really a city within a city.*

## THE OLD CITY

At the time of Jahangir and Shah Jahan, Agra was one of the great cities in the world, famous for its commercial activity and military strength. As traveller Ralph Fitch wrote in 1584, *'Agra is a very great citie and populous ... it hath a faire castle ... either one of them (Agra and Fatehpur Sikri) much greater than London.'* During the reign of the Mughals, Agra was crowded and rich, with schools, bazaars, *hammams* (baths) and magnificent royal buildings. Walking around the Old City of Agra, one can see remains of this past here and there, but generally it is a crazily crowded area, congested with cows, cycle-rickshaws and ubiquitous Maruti cars edging through heaps of vegetables and flowers lying in open stalls along the road.

### Shopping in Agra

All sorts of merchandise can be found here, from dried fruit to walking sticks, kites and sweets. The Old City is a maze of narrow alleyways and it is very easy to get lost. The latest Bollywood songs blare out from shop fronts and directly opposite these are businesses selling washing machines and irons. Highly skilled craftsmen, working with dedication at their marble inlay work or *zardozi* (fabrics embroidered with gold or silver thread), line the streets. Descendants of the old master craftsmen still live among the ruined *havelis* and above the narrow streets. Kinari Bazaar is a good shopping area here, but watch out for overpriced poor-quality products. *Dhurries* are the speciality of Agra and the best shops are in the Old City in Johri Bazaar. Other Agra specialities are leather shoes, *gajak* (a sweet) and the famous *zardozi*. There are a number of jewellery shops and good *zardozi* work in **Kinari Bazaar**. Other markets include the **Loha Mandi** (iron

---

### SATI

*Sati* is the name for the practice in which widows jump into their husbands' funeral pyre and burn alive. Although it is strictly banned by the government, it continues in small villages in the interior of India to this day. Recently, a *sati* was committed in a village called Satpurva, outside Khajuraho. In 1987, when Roop Kanwar committed *sati* in Deorala in Rajasthan, the Prime Minister Rajiv Gandhi called it 'barbaric and reprehensible' and laws were formulated to ban the tradition. However, in places where traditional superstitions are still strong, *sati* continues to be viewed as ideal for the Hindu widow. Hundreds of women devotees are known to visit *sati* temples, because they believe that *sati matas* or (*sati*) goddesses) can cure childlessness and ill health.

market) and **Sabzi Mandi** (vegetable market). **Nai ki Mandi**, north of the Jama Masjid is the best place to find traditional leather shoes as well as *pietra dura* craftsmen. The work is slow and laborious and a small box can take up to a month to complete. The best place to find excellent *pietra dura* handicrafts is **Subhash Emporium** on Gwalior Road where they even have a book that contains specific *pietra dura* details of the Taj and can recreate them on demand.

### Jama Masjid

At the centre of old Agra, surrounded by clamorous markets, stands the **Jama Masjid** which Shah Jahan built for his eldest, most accomplished and favourite daughter **Jahanara**. This is Agra's busiest mosque and is jampacked on Fridays. Unlike other mosques four corners of the the Jama Masjid are not accented by tall minarets, but its dome is decorated with an eyecatching red sandstone and a white marble zig-zag pattern. Possibly because the mosque has been maintained by princesses, it has a special chamber reserved for women, and the water tank features a *shahi chirag* (royal stove) for heating water.

### AGRA CANTONMENT

Also known as Agra Cantt, it was built by the British in the 19th century. This area is typically British Raj with its wide avenues and now rather dilapidated bungalows. As you travel down Mall Road, it is easy to imagine colonial officials cycling to **Queen Mary's Library**

or **St George's Church**. Sadly, most of the cantonement buildings have been allowed to fall into disrepair, although some of them continue to be occupied by public offices and departments. St George's Church, designed by the architect JT Boileau, is a long building with a four storeyed tower, built in the familiar style of other churches in North India. **St John's College** is also worth a visit. It is regarded as one of the best educational institutions in North India and was built of red sandstone in imitation Fatehpur Sikri-style by Samuel Swinton Jacob.

## RAM BAGH

Across the Yamuna River, on the opposite bank of the Taj Mahal, you find the **Ram Bagh** (also Rambagh Garden of Rest and Paradise Garden). This first Mughal garden was created by Babur and laid out according to the *charbag* principles.

Being used to the cool greens of Persia, Babur was disappointed by the dry heat of India and wrote: '*One of the great defects of Hindustan is its lack of running waters, it kept coming to my mind that water should be made to flow by means of wheels wherever I might settle down, also that grounds should be laid out in an orderly and symmetrical form.*' He tried to recreate a similar landscape on the Indian plain. At Ram Bagh, the waterways intersect at a central point where a pavilion was built for the emperor. A complicated system of underground wells was dug to keep up a constant flow of water to the garden from the Yamuna. The garden is now just a shadow of its former self, the grass is parched and the fountains have run dry, but you can still admire the picturesque *charbagh* design.

**Opposite:** *Itimad-ud-Daulah's tomb, built by his daughter Nur Jahan.*
**Below:** *Veiled Muslim women at the Taj Mahal.*

## ITIMAD-UD-DAULAH'S TOMB

South from the Ram Bagh is the tomb of Itimad-ud-Daulah that has been described as a 'jewel box of marble'. It was built by Jahangir's queen, Nur Jahan for her father, Ghiyas Beg, a soldier of fortune who rose to prominence in Akbar's time and was given the title Itimad-ud-Daulah

(Lord Treasurer) by Jahangir. Historians have written that Nur Jahan had this tomb built in the grandest possible manner because she was anxious to affect a high monarchical style to hide her humble origins. A small structure, the tomb is astounding in the wealth of its carvings, mosaic, lattice and inlay work. It marks the transition from the no-nonsense red sandstone architecture of Akbar to the more refined, sensuous and delicate ornamentation of Jahangir and Shah Jahan. The flasks of wine patterned on the walls of the tomb have been interpreted as Nur Jahan's private joke on her alcoholic husband. They are a significant departure from Islamic architecture in which representations of wine are prohibited.

## CHINI-KA-RAUZA

North from Itimad-ud-Daulah, also overlooking the river, is the tomb of **Afzal Khan** known as **Chini-ka-Rauza** (China Tomb). Afzal Khan was a Persian scholar and important nobleman during the reign of Shah Jahan. This tomb was once covered with green and blue glazed tiles and decorated with verses from the Qur'an as well as the *pietra dura* patterns. Virtually nothing remains of the tiled façade, but the burial chamber still provides glimpses of the ornamental plaster patterns which were used to decorate tombs at this time.

---

### CHARBAGH

All the Mughal emperors loved gardens, so much so that the term Mughal Garden has entered the lexicon of Indian architecture to describe a geometrically planned lush area of land, decorated with pavilions and pools. *Char* means four, *bagh* means garden. *Charbagh* therefore indicates a garden plan that is divided into four squares (supposed to represent the four periods of life – childhood, adolescence, middle age and old age) by the axis of the central water canal. The first Mughal garden, created in Agra by Babur, was called the **Ram Bagh** or **Rambagh** and the *charbagh* principle was used in almost all Mughal tombs, including Humayun's in Delhi later copied by British architect Edwin Lutyens when he designed the viceroy's house in New Delhi, now become the presidential residence.

# Agra at a Glance

**Oct–Mar** is the best time to visit Agra. Minimum temperatures range from 19°C (66°F) to 8°C (46°F). Maximum temperatures are 35°C (95°F) to 23°C (73°F). By **mid-Sep**, the monsoon generally peters out across northern India. The weather in the Golden Triangle is cool and dry from Oct–Mar but winter mornings can be foggy and very cold. **Jan** can turn smoggy and chilly, and light rainfall is not uncommon.

### GETTING THERE

Agra is 223km (139 miles) from Delhi, with good road and rail links. A day trip on the air-conditioned **Shatabdi Express** departs from New Delhi at 06:00 and from Agra at 20:00; the journey takes about 2hr. **Indian Airlines** runs a daily air shuttle service from Delhi to Varanasi and Khajuraho via Agra. Buses from Delhi to Agra leave from the Inter State Bus Terminus. Luxury video coaches take 90 min and terminate at Idgah bus stand at Agra. Buses are crowded so it's best to use the train or the air service. Agra's **Kheria Airport** is 7km (4 miles) from town. Use a prepaid taxi at the airport or station rather than risk being overcharged. It's better to book through travel agents for coaches, trains or airlines. Hiring a car and driver for the day or several days can be surprisingly cheap, especially if

several of you share the costs.
**Jet Air**, Hotel Clarks Shiraz, Taj Road, tel: (0562) 222 6521-3.
**Indian Airlines**, Clarks Shiraz, tel: (0562) 222 6821.
**Airport information**, tel: (0562) 240 0569.
**Train information**, tel: 131 (computer enquiry system); (0562) 242 1039 (Cantt).

### GETTING AROUND

Cycle-rickshaws and prepaid taxis are the best way to get around, or arrange a rate for the full day on arrival. Do this from the hotel or via the tourist office to ensure a fair rate. Haji Tours and Travels, 435 Sultanpura, tel: (0562) 222 7938, mobile: 9837 253 172, is a reliable source of fixed price taxis and can also provide government approved guides.

### WHERE TO STAY

*LUXURY*
**Welcomgroup Mughal Sheraton**, Mall Road, tel: (0562) 233 1701, www.itc-welcomgroup.com Luxurious hotel in Mughal style, near Taj Mahal. Enclosed courtyards and gardens on a huge property. Excellent service, pool, health centre, fine restaurants including north-west frontier Peshawri, the poolside Bagh-e-Bahar, Taj Bano buffet, Mah Jong Chinese room, a coffee shop and a cocktail bar. Plus a compulsive shopping mall.
**Amarvilas**, Taj East Gate Road, tel: (0562) 223 1515, www.oberoihotels.com

Like a Mughal fort in its glory days, this hotel was built in traditional Mughal style, with every conceivable luxury.
**Agra Ashok Hotel**, 6B The Mall, tel: (0562) 236 1223, fax: (0562) 236 1620. A recently privatized hotel, clean but with a slightly municipal character. Large, comfortable rooms, courteous staff. Pool.
**Howard Park Plaza International**, Taj Ganj, Fatehabad Road, tel: (0562) 233 1872. A bit kitsch but very clean, with tip-top maintenance and an excellent poolside restaurant service.
**Clarks Shiraz**, Agra Cantt, 54 Taj Road, tel: (0562) 222 6121, www.hotelclarksshiraz.com India's first five-star hotel and one of Agra's oldest, now definitely overtaken by the opposition. The rooms are tired but have lovely views of the Taj Mahal; the food is adequate rather than good. Pool. This is tourist central with many useful offices and agencies on the premises.

*MID-RANGE*
**Hotel Mansingh Palace**, Fatehabad Road, tel: (0562) 233 1771, www.mansinghhotels.com Red sandstone building with lots of architectural details; airy, recently renovated rooms.
**Grand**, Agra Cantonement, tel: (0562) 222 7514.
**Hotel Atithi**, Fatehabad Road, tel: (0562) 223 0040, e-mail: hotelatithi@hotmail.com

# Agra at a Glance

**Amar Yatri Niwas**, Fatehabad Road, tel: (0562) 223 3030, fax: (0562) 223 3035, e-mail: amagra@sancharnet.in.
**Ganga Ratan**, Fatehabad Road, tel: (0562) 233 0329/0234.

### BUDGET

Most of the budget hotels are in Taj Ganj, a bustling area behind the Taj Mahal. There are plenty of cheap restaurants and hotels here, although this is the place where one needs to be on the look out for scams, pick-pockets and hotel rip-offs. The hotels are generally clean, the staff are friendly and can be helpful with organizing tours.

**Tourists Rest House**, Kachahari Road, Sadar Bazaar, tel: (0562) 236 3961, e-mail: dontworrychickencurry @hotmail.com Quiet, comfortable guesthouse, with garden, terrace and rooftop vegetarian restaurant, plus internet facilities; owner will organize tours. The same owners run the **Hotel Safari**, Shamsabad Road, tel: (0562) 233 3029.

Other budget hotels include:
**Bawa Palace**, Idagh Colony; tel: (0562) 242 0151.
**Sheela Hotel**, Eastern Gate, Taj Mahal, tel: (0562) 233 3074/1194.
**Hotel Sidhartha**, Western Gate, Taj Mahal, tel: (0562) 233 0931.

### WHERE TO EAT

Agra is not well known for fine dining. For safe, good-quality food, it's best to eat at the five-star hotels. The restaurants and bar at the Mughal Sheraton are the best, particularly for northwest frontier cuisine at the Peshawri. The Trident and Clarks Shiraz are good for sandwiches and kebabs.

**Dasaprakash**, Balu Ganj, off Gwalior Road, part of the all-Indian chain of Dasaprakash restaurants, provides the usual South Indian fare of *dosas*, *idlis* and South Indian coffee.
**Zorba the Buddha**, Osho Restaurant, off Gwalior Road, is run by the followers of the Rajneesh or Osho spiritual college. Vegetarian, very clean.
**Only Restaurant**, Mall Road, is typical of the eateries found in mid-sized towns of North India, offering wholesome, unpretentious meals. Garden tables. In the evenings, there is live Indian music.

### TOURS AND EXCURSIONS

The **UP State Tourism Development Corporation** offers daily tours of the Taj Mahal, Agra Fort and Fatehpur Sikri (10:15–18:15). Bookings through the tourist offices (*see* below). Local travel agents also offer a range of tours to Fatehpur Sikri, Bharatpur and Deeg, Sikandra, Mathura and Gwalior.
**TCI Travel Agency**, Clarks Shiraz Hotel; tel: (0562) 222 6521-3.
**UP Tourism** office, 64 Taj Road, tel: (0562) 222 6431; www.new7wonders.com
**Cantt Railway Station**, Agra, tel: (0562) 242 1204.
**Government of India Tourist office**, 191 Mall Road, tel: (0562) 222 6368. There are plenty of ATMs that accept foreign cards, if you need to change money.

### USEFUL CONTACTS

**District Hospital**, Mahatma Gandhi Rd, tel: (0562) 236 1099.
**Quick Silver Courier Service**, Block 43, Sanjay Place 2, tel: (0562) 252 1495.
**Cybercafé**, 1st Floor, Shree-Heera Plaza, Bypass Road.
**Archaeological Survey**, Mall Road, tel: (0562) 222 7261/3.
**Police**, tel: (0562) 233 1015 (Taj Ganj); (0562) 222 6561 (Sadar Bazaar).

| AGRA | J | F | M | A | M | J | J | A | S | O | N | D |
|---|---|---|---|---|---|---|---|---|---|---|---|---|
| AVERAGE TEMP. °C | 14 | 17 | 23 | 29 | 34 | 35 | 31 | 30 | 30 | 27 | 21 | 16 |
| AVERAGE TEMP. °F | 57 | 63 | 73 | 84 | 93 | 95 | 88 | 86 | 86 | 81 | 70 | 61 |
| HOURS SUN DAILY | 11 | 12 | 12 | 12 | 14 | 14 | 14 | 14 | 13 | 12 | 12 | 11 |
| RAINFALL mm | 25 | 22 | 17 | 7 | 8 | 65 | 211 | 173 | 150 | 31 | 1 | 5 |
| RAINFALL in | 1 | 0.9 | 0.7 | 0.3 | 0.3 | 2.5 | 8.2 | 6.8 | 5.9 | 1.2 | 0.04 | 0.2 |

# 6
# Around Agra

Only a small detour west of Agra will take you to the stunning ghost city of **Fatehpur Sikri**, once a seat of the Mughal empire under the free-thinking emperor Akbar. Even after seeing the Taj Mahal, this haunted city does not fail to impress. The **Keoladeo Ghana National Park** in Bharatpur, some 55km (34 miles) from Agra, is a must see for bird lovers, with over 300 species. The Water Palace in sleepy **Deeg** illustrates monsoon architecture beautifully. Landmarks **Mathura** and **Vrindavan** are famous for their connection with the Lord Krishna and for being busy sites of Hindu worship and pilgrimage.

## FATEHPUR SIKRI

If the Taj Mahal was Shah Jahan's signature and embodiment of the artistic and romantic aspects of his reign, then Fatehpur Sikri is Akbar's architectural autograph, built in his favourite red sandstone. Akbar was a tough empire builder and might have been impatient with the marble delicacies so favoured by his son and grandson. The buildings in Fatehpur Sikri are impressive and robust, but lack the finesse of later Mughal architecture. Akbar was engaged almost continuously in battles on all fronts to consolidate his empire. The architecture shows a fusion of the Islamic and Hindu styles. During the time that the city was being built Akbar was fighting with the rulers of Gujarat so several features of Gujarati architecture, such as the carved brackets in the Diwan-i-Khas (House of Private Audience), have been incorporated.

### DON'T MISS

**\*\*\* Fatehpur Sikri:** Akbar's 'City of Victory'.
**\*\*\* Keoladeo National Park:** a world heritage site, home to over 300 bird species.
**\*\*\* Water Palace at Deeg:** a breathtaking piece of Monsoon architecture (see page 113).
**\*\*\* Mathura and Vrindavan:** tour the temples and ghats in holy Krishna sites.
**\*\*\* Gwalior hilltop fort:** the views are incredible.
**\*\*\* Orchha:** a ghost town off the beaten track.

**Opposite:** *Entrance gateway to the Jama Masjid in Fatehpur Sikri.*

Fatehpur Sikri

**Key to Palace Complex**
1. Ticket Office and Entrance
2. Jodhai Bai's Palace
3. Lower Haramsara
4. Birbal's Palace
5. Maryam's Palace
6. Panch Mahal
7. Palace of the Christian Wife
8. Aankh Michauli (Treasury)
9. Diwan-i-Khas (Hall of Private Audience)
10. Pachisi Court with Ornamental Garden
11. Diwan-i-Am (Hall of Public Audience)
12. Rumi Sultana
13. Diwan Khana-i-Khas (Khwabgah)

It is believed that Akbar commissioned Fatehpur Sikri after his son was born. He had waited for a male heir for many years and was overjoyed when his Rajput wife gave birth to Salim, later called Jahangir, in 1569, a year after his annual pilgrimage to the Sufi saints at Ajmer. He was anxious to create a monument to his rule and bolster the prestige of the Mughal throne. Located 37km (23 miles) west of Agra, Fatehpur Sikri was built in 1571 and was the capital of the Mughal empire for 14 years.

Nobody knows why Akbar suddenly abandoned it, perhaps water supplies ran out or he was called away on a military campaign (*see* page 110).

The main entrance to the city is through the **Buland Darwaza** (Gate of Victory) built to commemorate Akbar's victory in Gujarat. It stands 54m (177 feet) tall and makes a medieval diving board for young men from the neighbouring village.

A section of the city houses the private quarters of the emperor, consisting of the **Khwabgah** (House of Dreams) sleeping quarters that overlook a lake called

Anoop Talao. It is a colonnaded building that was cooled by the breeze blowing in from the water. The emperor's wives came to him through latticed passages connecting his quarters with the harem.

The Anoop Talao or peerless Pool, set in the middle of a square, has a platform at the centre where Tansen, the legendary court musician sat. He was apparently such an accomplished musician that he was able to light lamps and create rainfall whenever he wished, through the sheer power of his voice. In a corner of the square is the small but exquisite pavilion of the Turkish sultana, one of Akbar's favourite wives. It could have served as a *hammam* or even as an informal discussion chamber. The elaborate carvings of pomegranates, palms and fabulous animals betray mixed influences from Persia, Turkey and even China.

The public area consists of the treasury, the **Diwan-i-Am** (Hall of Public Audience) and the harem. Then there is the sacred area where the delicately carved marble tomb of saint Sheikh Salim Chishti (the only marble structure in the city) and the Jama Masjid stands. Another great gateway, decorated with characteristic *chhatris* (small pavilions), the **Badshahi Darwaza** separates the royal living quarters from the sacred area.

The largest open courtyard at Fatehpur Sikri is the **Pachisi Court**. This was apparently used as a giant chess board on which courtesans played the parts of chess pieces while the emperor watched and directed them from the overlooking Panch Mahal. The fantastic Panch Mahal is a large five-storeyed pavilion open to cool breezes on all sides. There are 176 columns, none of which are exactly the same

> **JODHAI BAI**
>
> By the age of 26, Akbar had assembled 300 wives and a harem of 5000 concubines and yet he had no heir. It was the Rajput princess, Jodhai Bai of Amber, who gave him his first son Salim, later to become the emperor Jahangir. To celebrate this event, Akbar ordered the construction of Fatehpur Sikri. He was so fond of Jodhai Bai that he shaved off his beard and stopped eating onions and garlic which, according to her, were 'inconvenient in kissing'. He also gave up beef so as not to offend her Hindu principles.

**Below:** *Emperor Akbar's Tomb in Sikandra 8km (5 miles) from Agra.*

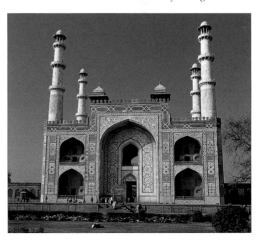

**THE MYSTERY
OF FATEHPUR SIKRI**

Only 14 years after its construction, Fatehpur Sikri was deserted forever. The entire court, including 1000 doorkeepers and 1200 horses, broke camp and abandoned the city to wild animals. It is not known what caused this sudden departure. Water shortage, military pressure on the northwest border of the kingdom, or the difficulty of maintaining two palaces (one each in Sikri and Agra), may have been the reasons. In the words of historian Richard Lannoy, Sikri was *'a tragic political failure'* but *'its failure has nothing to do with its architecture, which remains the most perfect expression of the liberal society which Indian rulers have vainly striven to realize.'*

and a superb view of the surrounding fields. In Akbar's time, there must have been a view of the river. The steps are rather steep and climbing them is certainly a calorie-burning exercise but must have been very pleasant in the evenings. The ladies of the harem sat out on the Panch Mahal on summer nights with their emperor.

The Diwan-i-Am and Diwan-i-Khas are the two main public halls of the city. The Diwan-i-Am is built like a large open courtyard where the emperor held his public hearings and occasional public prayers. This is also where he married his queen.

The **Diwan-i-Khas** (Hall of Private Audience) is a richly carved building, with interiors heavily influenced by Hindu styles. The curving staircase and the carved cross beams could easily pass for the interior of a Gujarati palace. The giant carved capital at the building's centre from which four walkways radiate towards a circular balcony, is a masterpiece. This is where Akbar sat

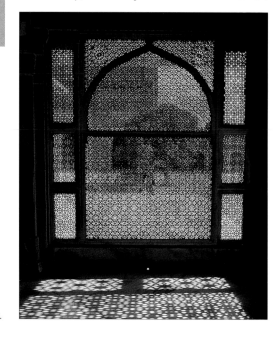

**Opposite:** *Akbar's unique Diwan-i-Khas overlooking the Pachisi Court.*
**Right:** *Sheikh Salim Chishti's tomb attracts crowds in search of a miracle.*

in his throne and surveyed his domain. The two-storeyed façade of the Diwan-i-Khas is square and boxy, with *chhatris* at either ends of the roof.

Yet another important public building is the **Aankh Michauli**, the treasury which stands behind the Diwan-i-Khas. The strange name comes from the story that the emperor played hide and seek here with ladies of the harem. Stone monsters guard the building's dark interior where the royal gold and silver was stored.

The **Jama Masjid** in the southwest corner is a huge open structure, with *chhatris* on its roof, delicate *jaali* work at either end and an open verandah lined with carved pillars.

To the west, the women's quarters or *zenana* include the main harem, several separate residences for the queens as well as a royal garden. The imposing **Jodhai Bai's Palace**, named after Akbar's favourite wife, was guarded by eunuchs and is where the emperor reputedly spent his nights. There is a section which was democratically converted into a temple for the Hindu contingent of the harem. The fusion of decorative styles is remarkable: we find elements of Gujarat and Gwalior art such as the blue tile work on the ceiling, mixed with Islamic details. The beautiful tulip motif is the city's blueprint.

**TROUBLE IN THE FAMILY**

Akbar's long-awaited son Salim was somewhat of a disappointment at first. Biding his time in the opulence of the court, Salim succumbed to debauchery, betraying his father's high aspirations, while his two younger brothers drank themselves to death. Akbar turned his attention to his grandson as a potential heir to the throne, thus inciting the bitter Salim to murder his father's gifted protégé and biographer Abu'l Fazl. Akbar arranged a fight between the elephants of his sons Salim and Khusrau. Salim's elephant won and shortly afterwards, the wayward prince became a capable emperor: Jahangir, 'Seizer of the World'.

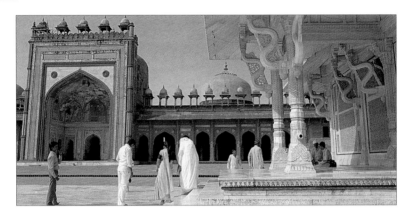

Across from Jodhai Bai's Palace, **Maryam's Palace** has obscure origins. It could have been named after a Christian queen, although there are no records to substantiate this claim. It is also possible that Akbar's mother lived here. The inside walls were once lined with gold frescoes depicting angels, birds and animals, hence the other name of the residence – **Sunahra Makan** (Golden House). There was an inscription on the wall once penned by Abu'l Fazl, the royal biographer: '*The gardens painted on these walls are on a par with the gardens of paradise*'.

It is a mystery why the third and finest main building of the *zenana*, **Birbal's Palace**, was named after Akbar's trusted advisor who could not have lived in the women's quarters. Birbal the Wise, the musician Tansen and the biographer Abu'l Fazl were three of the 'Nine Gems' at Akbar's court. This residence has preserved its intricate stone carvings of lotus blossoms and geometric forms.

Fatehpur Sikri is a ghost city today but at sunset when a red glow illuminates the ruins, you can imagine the life of the young and vigorous king: his harem, his debate hall, houses for his wives and mistresses, his mosque, the public buildings and the giant courtyard for his live chess games. Rich carpets and curtains adorned the palace, water flowed in its gardens and rose bushes lined the pools. Outside the city on the banks of the river Akbar is said to have played polo and watched his favourite sport: elephant fights.

> **MAKING A WISH AT CHISHTI'S TOMB**
>
> The tomb of the Sufi saint, Sheikh Salim Chishti, is an exquisitely carved marble structure inside Fatehpur Sikri. Legend has it that only after Salim Chishti had given emperor Akbar his blessings in the 16th century, Akbar's Rajput princess, Jodhai Bai, produced an heir thus ending his long period of childlessness. Ever since then hundreds have come to Salim Chishti's tomb to make a wish. The practice is to tie a thread on the marble screen around the tomb and hope for a miracle. Every day several new strings are tied to the screen, so the saint cannot be getting much eternal rest.

## KEOLADEO GHANA NATIONAL PARK

55km (34 miles) from Agra, the Bharatpur district is most famous for its Keoladeo Ghana National Park which includes a bird sanctuary. The town of Bharatpur was founded by Jat rulers in the 18th century. At its centre stands **Lohagarh Fort** (Iron Fort) which withstood many attacks from the bands of warriors who roamed this area after the decline of the Mughal empire.

The **Keoladeo Ghana National Park** in Bharatpur is a must-see. This once dry stony land was developed by Bharatpur rulers for use as a duck reserve. At the time duck shooting was a popular royal pastime – as many as 5000 birds could be shot in a single day. Today, the park is listed as a world heritage site and spreads over 29km$^2$ (11 square miles). It attracts over 300 bird species every year, including the Siberian crane, peregrine falcon, kingfisher, steppe eagle, different types of storks, herons and egrets. They can be seen crowding on islands in the water or flying out in a rush from the groves. Keoladeo has lovely walkways along the wetlands and bushes where the birds nest. You can either walk or cycle. There are also boats along the watercourses and cycle-rickshaws for hire. The park is open 06:00–18:00 daily, but the best time to see the birds is at dawn.

At the time of writing, Bharatpur has come under serious threat as a local water dispute is drying up the

**Opposite:** *The marble tomb of Sufi saint Chishti where wishes are granted.*
**Left:** *A nesting colony of painted stork at Keoladeo.*

wetlands and the birds are moving elsewhere. It must be hoped that the dispute is settled before this magical place becomes a desert.

## WATER PALACE AT DEEG

The tiny town of Deeg lies 98km (61 miles) north of Agra. It is not normally part of the tourist trail, but well worth a visit.

The rulers of Bharatpur loved the monsoon and the festivals associated with its dramatic arrival in northern India. The palace, built by the 18th-century ruler Raja Suraj Mal, is a breathtaking piece of architecture. It is an example of what is known as Monsoon Architecture – buildings designed to keep rooms cool by making use of the breeze and shutting out glare. The ingenious use of tanks, fountains and underwater cooling systems is exemplified by the palace at Deeg and shows how the architects dealt with the scorching heat of the Indian plains. The Water Palace overlooks two massive tanks, the Gopal Sagar and Rup Sagar. Water from these is diverted along waterways that are strategically placed throughout the palace complex. Nowadays the fountain jets on the waterways are only activated during the festival season. Two pavilions shaped like boats stretch out onto the main tank.

**Left:** *The Banyan Indian Fig Tree is a symbol of strength and endurance.*
**Opposite:** *Hindu Pilgrimage Site in Mathura.*

## MATHURA

Mathura, 62km (39 miles) from Agra, is the birthplace of Lord Krishna and as a result the surrounding towns are important centres of Hindu pilgrimage. The fact that these Hindu holy places continued to flourish right under the noses of the mighty Mughals who were proud Muslims, is a great tribute to the generally liberal policies of the emperors. This area is known as the *brajbhumi* and includes the towns of Vrindavan, Radhakund, Govardhan and Kosi.

Krishna, supposed to have been an incarnation of Vishnu, the Preserver, is one of the most popular Hindu gods. He is a blue skinned, flute-playing cow herder, much loved by the local ladies, who slew the evil King Kamsa and brought peace to his land. Krishna's birth is celebrated with an important festival called *Janmashtami*. It celebrates the birthday of Lord Krishna and takes place during the monsoon. It is best experienced in the temples of Vrindavan, 68km (42 miles) north of Agra. There is said to have been a fearsome rainstorm at Krishna's birth, to announce that 'the one who would destroy Kamsa' had been born. His father Vasudev carried baby Krishna across the Yamuna in a basket. The waters were so turbulent that Vasudev nearly drowned, but the great snake Sheshnag emerged from the river and spread its

### INDIAN TREES

There is an immense variety of trees in India and although deforestation is a major problem, trees have often been the objects of worship. The Peepul tree is considered holy as the Buddha is supposed to have attained enlightenment while he was meditating under it. The Ashok tree is also an extremely popular Indian tree, shaped in a bulge at the top. Other common trees are Banyan, Neem and Jamun. The Banyan is a mighty tree with roots dangling from the branches. It is a symbol of all that is strong and enduring. The Neem is a medicinal tree and it is a common practice among Indians to use its branches to clean their teeth. The Jamun or blackberry tree is seen all over Delhi and Agra and yields a tangy dark fruit.

**Above:** *Dancing* Nati's (*goddess*) *relief in the Government Museum.*

hood over father and child to shelter them. Krishna was a naughty child, terribly fond of dairy products, particularly *ghee* and butter. Paintings of a chubby blue child wearing a feather crown and gorging on butter are extremely common in Hindu households and shops all over north India. Krishna's consort is the beautiful Radha, whom he wooed with the music of his flute and finally married. Love stories of Krishna and Radha have inspired many poems and legends. One of the most famous is the *Geet Govind*. Krishna's name is synonymous with love and sweet romance in lush green gardens. Famous is the rather grim looking room in the **Sri Krishna Janmabhoomi Temple** (on the outskirts of the city of Mathura) which marks the spot where Krishna was born. Mathura is a colourful, constantly festive city with temples lining its *ghats*. The most famous is **Vishram Ghat** where Krishna is said to have come after killing Kamsa.

The Krishna legend is by no means Mathura's only claim to fame. From the 5th century BC Mathura was a centre of Buddhism and regarded as the premier north Indian city in terms of its artistic and scholarly achievements. The Mathura school of art is on display at the **Government Museum** (open from 10:30 to 16:30, Tuesdays to Sundays). The museum has stone scupltures and brass artifacts dating from ancient Indian dynasties. It also houses the headless statute of Kanishka, a conqueror who founded a huge empire with its capital at Peshawar in the 1st century AD. There is also a statue of the Standing Buddha and fragments of ancient palaces. The images at the Government Museum show traces of Greek influence after Alexander's invasion of India. The museum as a whole provides glimpses of the rich north Indian civilisation over the last centuries BC through the first centuries AD.

# VRINDAVAN

Vrindavan (Forest of Fragrant Basil) is where Krishna used to dance at Holi (the festival of colours) with Radha and her *gopis* (cowgirl consorts). The festival takes place between January and March and is celebrated on a full moon night towards the end of winter. People sprinkle coloured powder and water on each other, drink *bhang* (opium flavoured milk), dance and sing. The town is an important Hindu pilgrimage site.

Of the many important temples located in Vrindavan, the most notable is **Govindeoji Temple** built in 1590 by Raja Man Singh I of Amber. This temple is seven storeys high and every year thousands of Vaishnavite pilgrims (followers of Vishnu) come here to pray. The **Sri Ranganathji Temple** is architecturally similar to the temples of south India. It has a carved *gopuram* (a pyramidical pillar) at its summit. During festivals, the temples of Vrindavan are decorated with flowers, clay lamps and brightly coloured flags.

Since the early decades of the 20th century, traditional Hindu families sent their widows to holy cities like Vrindavan and Benares. Some of them were extremely young because it was common practice to marry young girls to much older men. The widows shaved their heads and wore simple white clothes as a mark of their widowhood. The custom of sending widows to Vrindavan has almost completely disappeared today, although widows are still sent to this city from very poor areas because their families can no longer look after them. They live in the temples or in *vidhva ashrams* (widow shelters) and are cared for by the temple administrators. The plight of the widows of Vrindavan and Benares is a subject of great social concern and many citizen groups are campaigning for improved living conditions for them.

**Below:** *The* Ghat *below Vishram Temple.*

## GWALIOR

Only 119km (74 miles) south of Agra in the province of **Madhya Pradesh** is the city of Gwalior which boasts, among other things, what is perhaps India's most fabulous hilltop fort. A little further south is sleepy Datia's fascinating palace and Orchha's hidden mysteries. This is a highly recommended detour which offers a concentrated dose of some of India's most spectacular architecture. They are slightly off the beaten track but this adds to their beguiling mystique. An extra day or two are needed to make this trip from Agra.

Despite being dusty and crowded, Gwalior is home to a major monument of Rajput genius and extravagance. The spectacular hilltop fort, known as 'the pearl in the necklace of the castles of Hindustan' is the finest of its kind and has a long and turbulent history. Spreading over a vast expanse of sandstone and comprising six palaces, it is accessed by car or rickshaw from the west or through a succession of gates in the northeast. The western road snakes through a gorge and offers views to the curious Jain rock sculptures. Enormous and solemn, these figures date from between the seventh and the 15th centuries and depict the 24 Jain teachers either sitting cross-legged with palms turned upwards, or standing rigidly. Towering over them is the 19m (62 feet) high sculpture of Adinath (the Hindu god, *Shiva*). There is a path leading up to the southeast entry of the fort, where another cluster of sculptures is found and where Jain worshippers leave offerings.

**Opposite:** *The detailed cenotaphs at Orchha.*
**Right:** *Gwalior Fort: the splendid façade of Man Mandir or Painted Palace.*

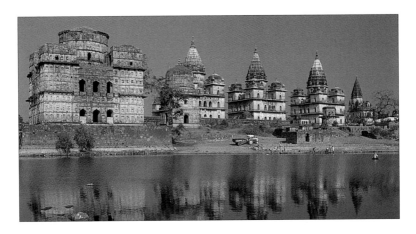

The fort dates as far back as the 10th century when **Kachhawaha Rajputs** ruled the region. The Rajputs were however soon crushed by a Delhi sultan. Rather than face the invaders, the women of the fort committed mass suicide in a huge water tank north of the main palace, legendary for its medicinal waters. In the 14th century the **Tomars** established a new era of Rajput domination and a splendid new palace was erected under the powerful ruler **Man Singh** in the late 15th century. The main building of this palace, **Man Mandir** (Painted Palace), boasts an exquisitely tiled exterior in turquoise, green and yellow depicting exotic animals and palm trees. Other buildings and temples in the enclosure can be explored on foot. It is best to **hire a guide** for an hour or two, who can provide interesting historical details – but be sure to settle on payment beforehand.

## DATIA

The magnificent seven-storeyed hilltop palace of Datia was built in the late 16th century by the eccentric Raja Bir Singh Deo, a friend of Prince Salim (later Jahangir). This is the other architectural wonder of India that was created by Lutyens, who also designed New Delhi. The fairytale palace offers fantastic views of the sleepy blue

---

### VIOLENCE AT GWALIOR FORT

The magnificence of Gwalior Fort is all the more awe-inspiring for the violence of its history. When the Delhi sultan ousted the Rajputs in the 13th century, the royal ladies committed suicide and 700 prisoners were executed outside the sultan's tent. During the 16th century the Lodi sultans from Delhi once again attacked the Rajput fortress. Man Singh was captured and killed as was his son, who had heroically resisted the Muslims for a year. The eight wives of Man Singh, after beheading a succession of Muslim intruders at the doorways of their swing room (where the king had installed eight swings for them), committed suicide by fire.

**Right:** *The royal suite at Hotel Sheesh Mahal in Orchha.*

and white-washed village below. Giant stone elephants adorn its top-storey façade, and a labyrinth of ascending passageways, *jaali* screens and bright tilework lead up to the delicate apartments of the queen which still retain their exquisite murals. This is where the Raja liked to sit, close to his Rani, look out at the great plains of his king-dom and write poetry. There are no opening hours as such, but the caretaker lives outside the main entrance and allows visitors in as they arrive. He also provides an entertaining tour of the palace and idiosyncratic inter-pretations of Rajput history.

## ORCHHA

This sleepy town, whose name means Hidden Place, casts a powerful spell on the visitor. The airy **Jahangir Mahal**, one of the most splendid palaces of Rajasthan, was built by local chief Raja Bir Singh Deo as a gift for a visiting allied emperor. Next door, the **Sheesh Mahal** (Mirror Palace) is a smaller palace doubling as a charm-ing government-run hotel with breathtaking rooftop views. A must-see are the remarkably well-preserved frescoes from the *Ramayana* at the isolated Lakshminarayan Mandir, a 20-minute walk through town, as well as the dreamy *chhatris* by the river. Ask at the Sheesh Mahal for a **walkman-guided tour** of Orchha if you are only staying for a day.

# Around Agra at a Glance

**Oct–Mar** is the best time to visit the Golden Triangle but in the Agra region it can be fairly hot even in Oct. **Dec–Jan** are preferable. Dec is also a good time to see Keoladeo Ghana National Park in Bharatpur. Maximum temperatures from **Nov–Feb** are 29°C (84°F) to 24°C (75°F); minimums are 12°C (54°F) to 10°C (50°F).

Roads around Agra are fairly well maintained, except for the dirt tracks leading to some of the smaller towns. The road to Bharatpur from the main highway is quite rocky and bumpy. Distances between Agra and the places around it are short and it is best to hire a taxi or chauffeur-driven vehicle, as the trauma of India's roads could test the hardiest driver. Most hotels have **chauffeur-driven tours** around the Agra region. Cars are not allowed within the park at Bharatpur; you can hire bicycles or cycle-rickshaws near the main gate and boats in the park. There are few taxis in the town, so if you want to explore the surrounding area, it is best to organize a car from Agra.

### Bharatpur
*MID-RANGE*
**Laxmi Vilas Palace Hotel**, Bharatpur, tel: (05644) 232 523; www.laxmivilas.com A heritage hotel in a renovated Rajput palace. Enclosed court-yard, wild swans on its lawns and a pool. The food is mostly *Mughlai*. Organizes excursions.
**Bharatpur Forest Lodge**, in the park, tel: (05644) 222 760, fax: (05664) 222 864. A comfortable hotel made special by its position inside the park, ready for birdwatching at dawn.

### BUDGET
**Hotel Sunbird**, Bharatpur, tel: (05644) 225 701; www.hotelsunbird.com (budget). Clean but fairly basic hotel near the park, run by enthusiastic, knowledgeable bird-watchers. Other budget hotels near the park include the **Spoonbill Hotel**, tel: (05644) 223 571; **Falcon Guest House**, tel: (05644) 223 815; **Jungle Lodge**, tel: (05644) 225 622.

### Mathura
**Radha Ashok**, tel: (0565) 253 0395, fax: (0565) 253 0396. Mid-range, but the best hotel in Mathura with air conditioning, friendly staff and a pool. **International Guest House**, tel: (0565) 242 3888. Good value, serves vegetarian meals.

### Vrindavan
**MVT Guesthouse**, tel: (0565) 254 0050; e-mail: mvt@com.bbt.se Pretty gardens, good restaurant with pizza, cake and ice cream besides Indian food. **The ISKCON** (International Society for Krishna Consciousness) **Guest House**, tel: (0565) 254 0022. Clean but spartan. Offers a good vegetarian *thali*.

### Gwalior and Orchha
**Ushan Kiran Palace**, Jayendraganj, Lakshar, Gwalior, tel: (0751) 232 3993; fax: 0751-232 1103. Raj-style hotel, lovely garden, excellent restaurant. **The Sheesh Mahal**, Orchha, tel: (07680) 252 624. A faded maharaja's palace, very good value for stunning rooms, good food in colonnaded hall and candle-lit rooftop dining.

Bharatpur offers painted miniatures of birds, available at the **Laxmi Vilas Palace Hotel**. In **Mathura** and **Vrindavan**, the markets are generally crowded with toys and *salwar kameez* (traditional Indian dress) sets. A large variety of delicious sweets is also available. Most popular is the *peitha* or candied pumpkin. You'll find incense, paintings, icons and replicas of temples.

**Alwar Tourist Information Office**, near the train station, tel: (0144) 221 868.
**Bharatpur Tourist Information Office**, opp. RTDC Hotel Saras, tel: (05644) 222 542.
**Bharatpur Wildlife Office**, Park Main Gate, National Highway 11, tel: (05644) 222777.
**Gwalior, Madya Pradesh Tourism**, Hotel Tansen (near station); tel: (0751) 234 0370.
**Mathura Tourist Information Office**, upstairs at old bus station; tel: (0565) 250 5351.
**Orchha, Madya Pradesh Tourism**, Hotel Sheesh Mahal.

# Travel Tips

## Tourist Information

There are tourist information offices run by central and state governments. For information, you may contact the overseas representatives of the Indian **Government Tourist Offices**. **Australia** (Sydney), tel: (02) 9264 4855, fax: (02) 9264 4860. **Canada** (Toronto), tel: (416) 962 3787, fax: (416) 962 6279. **Holland** (Amsterdam), tel: (020) 620 8991, fax: (020) 638 3059. **Singapore**, tel: (065) 235 3800, fax: (065) 235 8677. **South Africa**, tel: (011) 325 0880, fax: (011) 325 0882. **UK** (London), tel: (020) 7437 3677, fax: (020) 7494 1048. **USA** (Los Angeles), tel: (213) 380 8855, fax: (213) 380 6111; (New York), tel: (212) 586 4901-3, fax: (212) 582 3274. In Delhi, the **Government of India Tourist Office** HQ is 88 Janpath, tel: (011) 332 0005 or 332 0008, or **Delhi Tourism Development Corporation**, N-36 Connaught Place, tel: (011) 331 4229. The **Rajasthan state tourist office** in Delhi is in Bikaner House, Pandara Road (south from India Gate), tel: (011) 338 9525, and the Uttar Pradesh office in Chanderlok Building, 36 Janpath, tel: (011) 332 2251. Also check the website www.tourismindia.com

## Embassies and High Commissions in Delhi:

**Australia** tel: (011) 5139 9900; **Canada** tel: (011) 5178 2000; **New Zealand** tel: (011) 2688 3170; **South Africa** tel: (011) 2614 9411; **UK** tel: (011) 2687 2161; **USA** tel: (011) 2419 8000.

## Entry Requirements

You'll need a tourist visa which allows you to stay up to one, three or six months; The fee depends on the duration. Apply at your nearest Indian High Commission or Embassy with a travel itinerary and one or two passport photographs. If you're on a business trip, you will require a business visa, obtained in the same way. Allow at least a week for postal delivery, depending on location. Departure tax is Rs 750 (normally included in airfare).

## Customs

On arrival in India, you must declare a sum exceeding US $10,000 or any valuables, such as video cameras and laptops. Travellers over the age of 17 can import one bottle of wine and 250ml spirits, 200 cigarettes, 50 cigars, or 250g of tobacco. You can export handicrafts, but there are restrictions on antiques. It is illegal to export objects made from animal skin or ivory.

## Health Requirements

Although you need no health certificate to enter India, immunization prior to travel is essential, as is travel insurance. The basic vaccines are for typhoid, meningitis, hepatitis A, tetanus, diptheria and polio. A rabies jab is advisable only if you will be working with animals. Malaria, transmitted by mosquitoes, is widespread in India, especially during the monsoon season (July–August). Consult a doctor about the latest malaria tablets and remember to continue taking the tablets for four weeks after your trip, as malaria has an incubation period of a month.

## Getting There

**By air:** New agreements signed in 2005 have paved the way for greatly increased air services between India, the UK and the USA, including direct flights to many regional airports. Meantime Air India, British Airways and Virgin operate regular non-stop flights to Delhi. Prices can be brought down considerably by stopping en route. Amongst the cheapest options is Etihad, via Abu Dhabi. UK tel: (020) 8759 2111; Delhi tel: (011) 5152 8610/6; website: www.etihadairways.com

**By road:** The road from Europe passes through Turkey, Iran and Pakistan. Alternatively, you may take the Trans-Siberian Express to China and then travel southwest to India.

## What to Pack

Light, loose-fitting cotton clothing and **comfortable** footwear is essential. You may prefer closed sports shoes instead of sandals due to the dirt and dust on the streets. Avoid walking barefoot outdoors, unless you have to when visiting temples. Indians dress **conservatively**, especially women, and bare arms and legs, as well as tight pants, will attract stares. For both men and women, shorts should be a last resort. When entering temples, mosques and Muslim quarters, cover your legs and arms. Bring light winter clothing for the November–February period when it can be chilly, especially at night. Pack a raincoat for the monsoon months. For formal occasions and social gatherings, dress smartly – Indians are appearance-conscious and dress beautifully. Pack light, as you are likely to have excess baggage after a visiting all the interesting shops.

## Money Matters

The monetary unit is the rupee (Rs). There are a hundred paise in a rupee. You will mostly deal with banknotes, though there are coins too, starting at 5 paise and going up to 1, 2 and 5 rupees. Try to keep small change on you, as getting change back can be a hassle.

**Currency exchange:** The easiest currency to convert is US dollars, followed by the pound sterling. Travellers' cheques are safer than cash, and are generally accepted by **Thomas Cook** and **American Express** – provided they are in US dollars or pounds. To change cash, Thomas Cook, American Express or your hotel are hasslefree opportunities, and should take most currencies. There are plenty of ATMs with 24-hour access that take foreign cards.

**Credit cards:** Mastercard, Visa, American Express and Diners Club are accepted in most hotels, restaurants and shopping emporia. You can also pay for train tickets by credit card.

**Tipping:** *Baksheesh* is much practised. You are expected to tip porters, waiters, hotel staff and anyone else who delivers a satisfactory service. Ten rupees is the minimum but it is really up to you how much to give. Locals give beggars alms and joining in is the decent and appreciated thing to do.

**Tax:** Tax varies, but expect a 10 per cent tax on your hotel bill. You can always inquire before you check in and try to negotiate a better deal.

## Accommodation

The hotels recommended in this book are mostly mid- to top-range. Cheaper establishments have obvious disadvantages (lack of air conditioning, shared facilities and poor hygiene). Some hotels have air coolers that also do the trick. Most medium-priced hotels have reasonable in-house restaurants and room service. The main difference between mid- and top-range rooms, aside from the décor, is the mosquitoes – but this need only be a concern during the monsoon season (May–September). There are two types of top-range hotels. First, the Raj-style 'heritage' hotels – usually converted medieval palaces and *haveli*. The second type is the modern luxury hotel, often an international chain such as Oberoi, Meridien, Ashok and Claridges. The Taj Group of Hotels seek to emulate a Raj authenticity but are more business-like, although their grandeur is impressive. Most deluxe hotels have several top restaurants, a beauty salon, shops, pool, gym and a booking information service for tourists. Some even have good bakeries. Book in advance because the Golden Triangle attracts Indian as well as foreign visitors at all times.

## GOOD READING

- *India Magazine*, cultural monthly.
- **G Barton & L Malone** (1988), *Old Delhi: 10 Easy Walks*, Delhi.
- **W Dalrymple**, *City of Djinns*, London (highly readable account of a year spent in Delhi).
- **P Davies** (1989), *Penguin Guide to the Monuments of India*, Volume I & II, London.
- **G Devi** (1976), *A Princess Remembers: the Memoirs of the Maharani of Jaipur*, London.
- **R E Frykenberg** (1986), *Delhi Through the Ages*, New Delhi.
- **Kushurant Singh**, (1990), *Delhi: a Novel*.
- **V S Naipaul** (1990), *A Million Mutinies Now*, London (classic overview of Indian society, highly recommended).
- **M Tully** (1991), *No Full Stops in India*, London (BBC journalist's account of modern India).

# Eating Out

In India, you can eat very well on a small budget and lavishly on a large one. This part of India has an astonishing variety of foods, among which the heavy and exotic Mughlai cuisine, and of course, northern Indian food. Indian food of all kinds, but especially the wonderful and light South Indian dishes, is available in establishments ranging from very cheap and safe popular eateries to luxury hotel restaurants. Delhi is a gourmet's paradise and in addition to Asian and European cuisines, it has many Western-style fast-food establishments like *Pizza Hut* and *McDonalds*. Jaipur has a selection of restaurants, though authentic Rajasthani food is not easy to come by. Agra is sadly lacking in this department – there are a number of good restaurants but not nearly enough to cater for the demand. Most of Delhi's finest restaurants are in luxury hotels and in the residential districts of New Delhi.

# Transport

**Air:** Air travel is ideal for those with very limited time, but it foregoes the wonderful experience of seeing the countryside that land travel provides. There are regular flights from Delhi to both Agra and Jaipur with **Indian Airlines**, tel: (011) 2462 0566, general enquiries, tel: 141, departures, tel: 1403; and Jet Airways, tel: (011) 5164 1414. The domestic airport is 15km (9 miles) southwest of the city; Enquiries, tel: (011) 2569 6021.

**Road:** Exploring the Golden Triangle by car is definitely the best way to do it. There are two options: hiring a self-drive car or a chauffeur-driven vehicle. The first is slightly cheaper and can be done through any of the international companies like **Hertz** or **Budget**, or through a travel agent or tourist office. This option is not recommended, however, Indian roads are dangerous and have a high death toll. The second, safer, option involves taking a driver along, who might offer further insights into some of the things you come across on your trip. Book through a tourist office, travel agent, or at your hotel.

**Rajasthan Tourism Development Corporation**, Bikaner House, Pandara Rd, tel: (011) 2338 3837.

**Buses:** Buses are a good, safe substitute for a car. Although there are state-run buses, if comfort is a priority use the luxury buses run by private companies and hotels. Book through any travel agent (see above) or at your hotel.

**Trains:** Trains are efficient, even if crowded, and are recommended for long-distance travel. They are also a fast way to get around the Golden Triangle if you don't want to stop on the way; ideal for direct trips from Delhi to Jaipur and Agra. The best train journeys are:

**Delhi-Agra** on the Shatabdi Express, departs 06:00 (2 hours) from New Delhi railway station or the Taj Express, departs 07:15 (2 hours 30 minutes) from Hizrat Nizamuddin.

**Delhi-Jaipur** on the Shatabdi Express, departs 06:00 (4 hours 15 minutes) from New Delhi railway station, or Ahmedabad Mail, departs 22:50 (5 hours 25 minutes). For overnight journeys, book a second- or first-class sleeping wagon. There are three main railway stations – **New Delhi Station**, **Delhi Station** in Old Delhi and **Hizrat Nizamuddin**. For bookings, tel: 1330/35/45, www.indianrail.gov.in Book second or first class. The famous trip in the **Palace on Wheels** is in its own class. It departs every week from Delhi, and goes through

Jaipur, Udaipur, Jaisalmer, Jodhpur, Bharatpur and Agra. Prices are hefty, but the itinerary is exceptional. For bookings, UK tel: (0124) 858 0600; USA tel: (212) 920 2543; India tel: (0877) 463 4299; website: www. palaceonwheels.net

**Taxis:** Taxis are cheap and readily available. In Delhi and Jaipur they are painted black and yellow. In congested traffic, auto rickshaws are faster and even cheaper, although you get more of the pollution. Cycle rickshaws are unstable in traffic, but a splendid way to see the narrow streets of Old Agra and Old Delhi. This experience is compulsory – and safe. Negotiate payment before you set off, or have the driver turn on the meter. You should tip the cycle-rickshaw driver.

## Business Hours

**Shops:** Shops are open 09:30–18:00, Monday–Saturday. Markets have longer hours. On Sunday shops and most markets are closed. Some shops have individual trading hours.

**Offices:** Government tourist offices open from 09:30–17:00, Monday–Friday and from 09:30–13:00 Saturday. Saturday is a working day in India.

**Pharmacies:** There are 24-hour pharmacies in most cities. Ask at your hotel.

**Post Offices:** From 10:00–17:00, Monday–Friday and until noon on Saturday.

## Time

All of India is five and a half hours ahead of Greenwich Mean Time.

| CONVERSION CHART | | |
|---|---|---|
| **FROM** | **TO** | **MULTIPLY BY** |
| Millimetres | Inches | 0.0394 |
| Metres | Yards | 1.0936 |
| Metres | Feet | 3.281 |
| Kilometres | Miles | 0.6214 |
| Square kilometres | Square miles | 0.386 |
| Hectares | Acres | 2.471 |
| Litres | Pints | 1.760 |
| Kilograms | Pounds | 2.205 |
| Tonnes | Tons | 0.984 |
| To convert Celsius to Fahrenheit: x 9 ÷ 5 + 32 | | |

## Communications

**Telephones:** The international code for India is 91, followed by the local code (with a zero for national calls) – 11 for Delhi, 141 for Jaipur, and 562 for Agra. You can make direct or operator-assisted calls to any country. Collect and credit card calls to some countries such as the USA, UK, Ireland, Canada, Australia, New Zealand among others are possible. In cities, you will see STD booths (Standard Trunk Dialling) where you can call any national or international destination for a fee considerably smaller than at your hotel – it is calculated by the second. Some booths are open night and day. Most hotels have fax facilities, as do the STD booths. GSM mobile phones work and coverage is excellent. Visitors from North America will need a tri-band phone.

**Post:** Post to and from India is generally reliable but it can be slow. Buy your stamps at the post office and hand your mail over the counter rather than put it in a letterbox. Sending a parcel is a convoluted affair – parcels have to be stitched into cotton cloth, wax-sealed, custom-cleared, and are best registered. This can be done for you at larger post offices. Printed matter can be sent more cheaply as 'book post'. For speed, use a courier firm.

**Media:** There are some good-quality English-language newspapers; among these are: *The Hindu*, *Times of India*, *The Independent* and *The Indian Express*. Magazines of substance are *India Today*, *Outlook* and *The India Magazine* (cultural events).

## Electricity

Power supply is 220V, 50Hz. For sensitive appliances, use a stabilizer (available at larger hotels). The plugs are European-style with three round pins (two-pin plugs are fine too).

## Weights and Measures

The metric system is used. Gold and silver are sold by 11.5 grams, or *tola*. Precious stones are weighed in carats (0.2g). In Statistics *lakhs* and *crores* are used. A *lakh* is 100,000 units and a *crore* is 100 *lakhs*.

## Health Precautions

It is advisable to pack a survival kit consisting of salt powder (also widely available in India as electrolyte), that also guards against dehydration in summer; antibiotics; aspirin; throat lozenges; allergy medication; antiseptic cream; band-aids; insect repellent, sun-block, antibacterial towels and gel. Visitors to India may experience short-term intestinal trouble, also known as **Delhi-belly**, due to the novelty of the food and water, combined with the heat. But if you take the following precautions, you should be fine: for the first few days eat simple food such as South Indian *thali* (platter), yoghurt, bread and rice. **Tap water** is unsafe. Drink only mineral or filtered water (sold at street kiosks in hotels and restaurants) and bottled soft drinks. Check the seal on mineral water bottles. Brush your teeth with mineral or filtered water too. Avoid ice cubes in your drinks. Steer clear of fresh vegetables, salads and cut fruit. Peel uncut fruit. Avoid street vendors – eat in restaurants and cafés where the food is freshly cooked. Avoid seafood. To ward off heat exhaustion, drink plenty of fluids, use sun-block and wear a hat. If you do succumb to the heat, rest in a cool room and drink lots of fluids. To prevent heat rash use talcum powder and wear loose-fitting cotton clothing. Avoid mosquitoes if possible – wear insect-repellent, especially in the evenings, and cover your legs and arms. In Delhi, mosquitoes don't generally carry malaria outside the monsoon season. During the monsoon and outside of Delhi however, take malaria pills. Stay away from dogs, monkeys and cattle. Wash your hands frequently – if water is unavailable on the road or while sightseeing, use antibacterial towels or antibacterial gel.

## Health Services

If you need a doctor, enquire at your hotel.
**Hospitals:** All-India Medical Institute of Medical Sciences, Ansari Nagar, Sri Aurobindo Marg, New Delhi, tel: (011) 2656 1123. Open 24 hours.
SMS Hospital, Sawai Ram Singh Rd, Jaipur, tel: (0141) 256 4222.
District Hospital, MG Road, Agra, tel: (0562) 236 3043.

## Safety

You are unlikely to be pick-pocketed in Delhi or Jaipur, though try not to carry large amounts of cash on you and leave your passport in the hotel. Women are safe but should keep their legs and shoulders covered.

## Emergencies

Police, tel: 100 (national). Also ask at your hotel.

## Etiquette

Remove your shoes before entering a temple or mosque, as well as some private homes. In mosques, if admitted, women cover their heads. Use your right hand for eating, shaking hands or

| USEFUL HINDI PHRASES |
| --- |
| *namaste* • **greetings, hello** |
| *dhanyavaad* • **thank you** |
| *kitna hai* • **how much** |
| *davai ki dukaan* • **medicine shop** |
| *paani* • **water** |
| *teekha* • **hot (as in chilli)** |
| *nahin chahiye* • **I don't want** |
| *maaph kijiye* • **sorry** |
| *kidhar hai* • **where is it** |
| *khana* • **food** |
| *garam* • **hot (as in oven)** |
| *thanda* • **cold** |
| *theek hai* • **okay** |
| *kal* • **tomorrow** |
| *parso* • **day after tomorrow** |
| *jaao* • **go away** |
| *nahin* • **no** |
| *achcha* • **nice** |
| *achcha laga* • **I liked it** |
| *ganda* • **dirty** |
| *han* • **yes** |

pointing, as Indians use the left hand to wash in the lavatory. Ask people before photographing them, as some dislike it. Some Muslim women cover their faces when photographed or turn their backs. Check before taking photos inside places of worship. Public displays of intimacy between men and women are not acceptable in Indian society.

## Language

There are 15 official languages in India, of which Hindi, English and Urdu are most common. In urban areas most people speak at least basic English, but this is not the case in the countryside and in provincial towns. A few words of Hindi will take you a long way.

# INDEX